A TOUR OF THE
CATHOLIC CATECHISM

A TOUR OF THE CATHOLIC CATECHISM

Fr. Peter Stravinskas

Marytown Press
1600 West Park Avenue
Libertyville, Illinois 60048-2593
847-367-7800

NIHIL OBSTAT
James P. Campbell, D. Min.
Censor Deputatus
January 17, 1996

IMPRIMATUR
Most Rev. Raymond E. Goedert, M.A., S.T.L., J.C.L.
Vicar General
Archdiocese of Chicago
January 19, 1996

ISBN: 0-913382-63-9
LCCCN: 95-075988

TABLE OF CONTENTS

FOREWORD

T en years ago now, Bernard Cardinal Law of Boston rose to the floor of the Extraordinary Synod of 1985 in Rome and voiced his suggestion that the Church produce a full compendium of Catholic doctrine as a way of solidifying the teaching of the Second Vatican Council and ensuring its full and proper implementation. That recommendation met with strong support from the Synod Fathers in general and from Pope John Paul II in particular. This was the case because so many bishops realized the confusion that existed in their local churches, not as a result of Vatican II's implementation but due to faulty renderings of its teachings and even outright misrepresentations.

As soon as the French edition of the *Catechism of the Catholic Church* appeared and many months before the English text was available, Fr. Peter Stravinskas embarked on a year-long series in the *National Catholic Register* to introduce readers to this new and exciting work of catechesis and evangelization, one that our Holy Father has termed "a sure norm" for transmitting and inculcating that "Faith which was once for all delivered to the saints" (Jude 3). Father Stravinskas brought to the task not only his professional expertise as a theologian, an educator and a writer—but also his skills as a parish priest.

I followed that series with interest and pleasure, especially since almost nothing else had yet surfaced at that early date. I found the material to be a faithful summary of the catechism, at once readable and accessible to the Catholics we find in our pews week in and week out. And so, I was delighted to learn that Marytown Press of Libertyville, Illinois, had undertaken to publish that series in book form, especially since not a few commentaries on the catechism have emerged of late that actually do violence to both the letter and the spirit of that crucial and authoritative document of the Church.

What do we have here? First of all, Father Stravinskas offers us a high-flying overview of the entire *Catechism of the Catholic Church*, paying particular attention to areas of special interest and need to the Church in the United States. He is well qualified to do this because of his extensive travel and the vast correspondence he receives from the whole country in his capacity as editor of *The Catholic Answer*.

Second, the reader can rest assured that the theology reflected here is not skewed in one direction or another. At one point in the work, Father Stravinskas notes that some potential readers of the catechism might be inclined to ask just whose theology would be discovered there: "Would it reflect the thoughts of Hans Kung or Marcel Lefebvre?" He summarized the situation well by saying that "the answer is that it reflects the faith of the Catholic Church as that has been known, loved and accepted from time immemorial." I think one can say the same about his commentary.

Third, the style of the work is such that any number of possible audiences could benefit: students in Catholic high schools or colleges; participants in RCIA or adult education programs. These will certainly appreciate the discussion questions found at the end of each section. Furthermore, individuals desirous of gaining a deeper grasp of the catechism and the faith enshrined in it will also benefit from this guided tour; preachers should likewise see in this a handy summary of the principal teachings and their practical application for our people.

The publication of this volume during the thirtieth anniversary of the conclusion of the Second Vatican Council is especially fortuitous, in my judgment, for I am convinced that this work will lead readers to plumb the depths of the catechism in a manner that will ultimately lead them to a true integration of the Council's goals and objectives into their lives as believers on the brink of the third millennium.

MOST REVEREND ELDEN F. CURTISS
ARCHBISHOP OF OMAHA

PREFACE

What a great privilege it is to be able to share with you my reflections on the *Catechism of the Catholic Church*. My hope is that this presentation will serve as an introduction that will whet your appetite to savor the full menu now that the text has finally appeared in English. I am convinced you will be personally enriched by the beauty and depth and insight of this landmark document, and you, in your turn, will enrich the lives of those you touch through your various apostolates.

Before allowing the reader to move on, I should like to thank in particular two individuals who played key roles in this endeavor.

As I was preparing this commentary for publication in weekly installments for the *National Catholic Register*, I received great incentive for this project from Nicholas L. Gregoris who, as a college seminarian living in my rectory, offered encouragement and valuable suggestions to improve and clarify the text; when the series neared completion, it was Nicholas who urged me to pursue the compilation of the work for an even wider audience. This son of mine in the Lord, of whom I am so proud, is now in his final period of preparation for Holy Orders studying in the Eternal City. May these months be a time of great grace and blessing.

A second collaborator must also be acknowledged, Miss Catherine Cook, who has served as my trusted and most competent administrative assistant for nearly a decade now. Without her tireless and selfless efforts, this project would have had difficulty in seeing the light of day. Cathy's loyal friendship and firm faith must be noted as well, both of which have been a source of great personal inspiration.

Now, let us begin our tour of the catechism.

introduction:
WHY A CATHOLIC CATECHISM?

My people perish for lack of knowledge.
Hosea 4:6

introduction:
WHY A CATHOLIC CATECHISM?

A ll is not well in the Church, especially in the developed countries—and hasn't been for five or six decades in many instances. What is the root cause of the problem? When different people are asked, they offer various responses. Some will suggest that the liturgical reform has brought us to the brink of disaster—or even beyond; others maintain that the Council itself was responsible. But these responses do not take into account the desolation of most of western Europe years before such events. Sacred Scripture, however, says, "My people perish for lack of knowledge" (Hosea 4:6). Not by accident, then, did Pope John Paul II appear almost "driven" to have produced the *Catechism of the Catholic Church*, as a kind of "first-fruits" of the Second Vatican Council. He firmly believes that this is the most necessary step to ensure the genuine and complete renewal of the Church envisioned by the Church's latest council. How so?

The human person is so constructed by Almighty God that the life of faith is possible only when one is brought to a knowledge of God and then confronted with the possibility of belief.

Faith, to be a truly human act, requires the assent of the mind to the truths revealed by God (and communicated by human agents), indeed the Truth of God found in the Person of Jesus Christ and faithfully and most fully preserved and transmitted by his holy, Catholic Church. Once the Catholic Faith is presented, an individual is then capable of making a decision for or against it, but not until then.

Educational psychologists speak of the pedagogical process as embodying cognitive and affective elements, and rightly so. In recent years, reacting to some excesses of the past, many religious educators have sought to balance the budget by avoiding what they consider to be "too much content" in favor of a more experiential approach. The result has been less than successful. Objective tests and even public opinion polls confirm the religious illiteracy not only of children and adolescents, but also of adults who have begun to lose hold of the truths of faith once imparted to them and now being lost for want of positive and ongoing reinforcement. Catechesis, the Holy Father reminds us in *Catechesi Tradendae* (1979), is not "kid stuff"; rather, it "is an education in the Faith of children, young people and adults, which includes especially the teaching of Christian doctrine imparted, generally speaking, in an organic and systematic way, with a view to initiating the hearers into the fullness of Christian life" (n. 18).

If the Pope's understanding of catechesis were in place, Gallup would not have been able to inform us that 70% of Catholics who receive Holy Communion every Sunday do not believe in Christ's Real Presence in the Eucharist; teenagers would not think that the four evangelists are a rock group; children would know their basic prayers, be able to recite the Ten Commandments and list the seven sacraments. An accurate and complete presentation of Christian truth is the linchpin of

Catholic life. If the Faith is not known and accepted, liturgy makes no sense (after all, who is being worshipped and why?); morality is neither possible nor even desirable (since few know how the Faith is to be lived and yet fewer have any rationale for living some of the hard truths of Christianity).

The prologue of the new catechism makes the point that "periods of renewal in the Church are also intense moments of catechesis," citing the patristic period with the great catechetical bishops like Sts. Cyril of Jerusalem, John Chrysostom, Ambrose and Augustine as leading the way. It likewise notes that "the ministry of catechesis draws ever fresh energy from the councils," with the Council of Trent and its subsequent *Roman Catechism* offered as a prime example of the connection between conciliar teaching and catechetical presentation brought together by people like Sts. Peter Canisius, Charles Borromeo, Turibius of Mongrovejo and Robert Bellarmine. Just how successful their efforts were can be seen from the fact that both Trent and the *Roman Catechism* served the Church so admirably for over four centuries.

New times and new situations, however, call for new ways of teaching the old, perennial truths. We have nothing from Trent to say about nuclear war, genetic engineering or even artificial contraception. The *Roman Catechism* cannot help us determine how the believer today should view contemporary developments in Scripture study, like form or redaction criticism, for the simple reason that such methods did not exist in the sixteenth century.

Pope Paul VI realized this and so commissioned the *General Catechetical Directory* (1971). The universal Church took cognizance of the centrality of catechesis in the life of the Church in the 1974 synod on evangelization and particularly that of 1977 on catechesis, and in a special manner with the follow-up apostolic exhortations: *Evangelii Nuntiandi* (1975) and *Catechesi Tradendae*. The extraordinary synod of 1985 (dedicated to an analysis of the post-conciliar period), however, zeroed in on the situation most directly, expressing the desire "that a catechism or compendium of all Catholic doctrine regarding both faith and morals be composed." And no one has been more enthusiastic and supportive in bringing that hope to fruition than John Paul II.

Seven years after the fact, the new catechism is a fact of ecclesial life, even if its arrival has not been achieved by a direct route. Voices of opposition were raised from the outset about the very acceptability of any kind of catechism in this "new age" of the Church since its publication would serve as an implicit declaration that there is a firm content of Christian faith today. Others doubted that one book could serve a truly universal Church, with the diversity of cultures that is part and parcel of Catholic life today and unknown in previous ages. Yet others wondered whose theology would be enshrined in such a document; would it reflect the thoughts of Hans Kung or Marcel Lefebvre? The answer is that it reflects the faith of the Catholic Church as that has been known, loved and accepted from time immemorial, offering to those seeking the truth today "the faith which comes to us from the apostles," as the Roman Canon puts it. And because that Faith transcends space and time, although obviously communicated in human categories, it is indeed possible to make a compendium that cuts across cultural differences. If that were not possible, we would have to admit that the possibility of the Catholic Church had also ceased to exist since no ecclesial unity can exist apart from a unity of faith.

Whom does the catechism consider to be its primary audience? The prologue answers the question succinctly: "This work is intended primarily for those responsible for catechesis: first of all the bishops, as teachers of the faith and pastors of the Church. It is offered to them as an instrument in fulfilling their responsibility of teaching the People of God. Through the bishops, it is addressed to redactors of catechisms, to priests, and to catechists. It will also be useful reading for all other Christian faithful." It is important to observe the stress on bishops here: They are the primary audience and, through them, it is presented to all other interested parties. In other words, in large measure, the future of this document rests with bishops— not in a body but in their individual dioceses as they oversee the religious education of the souls entrusted to their care—a responsibility they cannot bypass or delegate, even though they must share the task with others. Bishops are the indispensable link in the catechetical chain.

And what are the sources for the catechism? Again, the prologue provides us with a ready response: "Sacred Scripture, the Fathers of the Church, the liturgy, and the Church's Magisterium." Just how this works out in reality is demonstrated by a glance at a few pages of the text: On one page we find reference to Vatican II's *Gaudium et Spes*, the Gospel of Matthew, Genesis, Psalm 105, St. Augustine's *Confessions* and one of his sermons, Romans, Acts, Wisdom; the following page cites *Gaudium et Spes*, St. Thomas Aquinas' *Summa Theologiae*, Vatican I's *Dei Filius*, Vatican II's *Dei Verbum*, Genesis, Pope Pius XII's *Humani Generis*. Thus, as can be seen quite easily, the catechism encompasses the entire Tradition of the Church. A welcome inclusion is a healthy dose of excerpts from the writings of the great masters of Catholic spirituality.

A final note is that "it is intended as a point of reference for the catechisms or compendiums that are prepared in the various regions" (Final Report of 1985 Synod of Bishops). Hence, the foreseen impact is total. Providing "the meat and potatoes" for religious educators, it is also foreseen as the standard by which to compose and judge all texts designed for religious education. Catechetical series, then, that fail to incorporate the fullness of truth contained in this catechism, are to be judged unworthy of continued use or adoption.

Some observers of contemporary Catholic life have suggested that we should not over-emphasize the "head" to the exclusion of the "heart" in catechesis, and that is correct. Our problem for at least twenty-five years, however, has been that we have nearly excluded the head. Most of our people are involved in birth control, abortion, divorce and remarriage; or miss Sunday Mass and neglect of the Sacrament of Penance, not because they are evil or bad-willed (heart) but simply because they honestly no longer know the truth (head). And so, St. Paul instructs his converts not to have the *heart* of Christ, but to have the *mind* of Christ and to be transformed by the renewal of one's mind and not one's heart (cf. 1 Cor 2:16; Rom 12:2), which only makes sense for one who seeks to follow the Jesus who declared before the cynical Pilate, "For this was I born and for this I came into the world, to testify to the truth. Everyone who belongs to the truth listens to my voice" (Jn 18:37).

Simply put, the heart can only be reached when the head is on straight; that happens when the truth is conveyed and accepted.

The Catechism's Structure

The structure of the *Catechism of the Catholic Church* follows the basic outline of catechisms from time immemorial, that is, a breakdown into what sociologists refer to as creed, code and cult, or what theologians identify as dogma, morality and liturgy. A final section of the catechism provides a reflection on the meaning of prayer in general and the Lord's Prayer in particular.

The Holy Father speaks of these four areas as the "pillars" of the work. Why? Because the whole edifice is built on these foundational pieces. We believe certain things about the Triune God and the Church he established; these saving truths are then celebrated within the believing community, at the very same time serving as sources of strength to increase our faith; finally, what is believed through faith and brought to prayer is then lived in one's day-to-day experience, enabling a person of faith to show forth even here on earth the beatitude to which we are called through Baptism.

It is good that the catechism maintains the traditional fourth part on prayer and the Our Father, if for no other reason than the fact that so few people today have any real notion of what prayer is and how to do it, let alone being able to plumb the depths of something so profound as the Lord's Prayer. This section should help readers come to appreciate the difference between "praying" and "saying prayers."

The Pope notes that the work "is conceived as an *organic presentation* of the Catholic faith in its entirety" (emphasis in original). Perhaps one of the most serious lacunae in post-conciliar catechesis has revolved around this very point—the lack of cohesiveness. Bits and pieces may have been communicated, but not in any unified manner, with the result that those under instruction never came away with a complete picture of how everything is interrelated. The situation puts one in mind of a mosaic artist who throws all the tiles for a composition on the floor and tells onlookers that it's a depiction of an English countryside. Even the most imaginative souls would be hard-pressed to envision that; the artist must do the organizing if he wants the image to be perceived. The same is true of catechesis, and the catechism is intent on doing just that, and in aiding catechists to do that, too.

A TOUR OF THE CATHOLIC CATECHISM

Since the work is written in this way, the Pope urges that it "be read as a structured whole." In other words, the first time around the reader should plow through the volume from front to back (and it's not always easy reading). Later on, one may return to specific parts for a deeper understanding of what was only partially comprehended on the first try. Further, the catechism is a reference tool, which means that individual topics can be looked up in order to obtain a succinct answer to a particular question.

This work is "user-friendly" in a variety of ways, especially in its layout and use of typefaces: "The use of small print in certain passages indicates observations of an historical or apologetic nature, or supplementary doctrinal explanations. The quotations, also in small print, from patristic, liturgical, magisterial or hagiographical sources, are intended to enrich the doctrinal presentations." The catechism encourages readers to find the original and complete scriptural passages, especially when only summarized in the text. Perhaps the most valuable aspect of each chapter, however, is the "In Brief" conclusions or summaries, which encapsulate the principal truths conveyed. This feature is helpful for those who want only a thumbnail sketch of a discrete theological tenet and also offers bite-size statements of faith, for (let's say the bad word!) memorization. And yes, contrary to many self-styled religious education experts in this country, the catechism holds that certain basic facts should "be committed to memory."

Not surprising is the recognition that adaptation of this material will be necessary, "required by the differences of culture, age, spiritual maturity, and social and ecclesial situations among those to whom it is addressed. Such indispensable adaptations are the responsibility of particular catechisms, and, even more, of those who instruct the faithful." Some people, gun-shy and battle-weary over American efforts to neutralize Roman documents, may become nervous with that realization. As if to anticipate such a reaction, the present catechism cites the preface from the *Roman Catechism* of the Council of Trent to the same effect. Granted, good adaptation is like walking a tightrope, but simply because something is dangerous does not mean it cannot or should not be attempted; in fact, without adaptation, the catechism (as excellent as it is) will be a dead letter for the vast majority of Catholic faithful. It is the obligation and privilege of those concerned with catechesis to digest its contents and then to present its message in such a manner that people of different backgrounds will be able to understand and appreciate its salvific message. It is also the responsibility of local bishops to ensure that adaptations (whether in textbooks or in catechist workshops) are truly faithful to both the letter and spirit of the original work.

In an age so given to ideology and so highly politicized, the present catechism again leans on the *Roman Catechism* of Trent to remind all of what we should be about: "The whole aim of doctrine and teaching must be put in the context of that love that never ends. No matter how clearly we may explain what we must believe, hope or do, we must first and always make the love of the Lord so apparent that all may understand that every act of perfect Christian virtue has no other origin and no other end than love." Those being catechized (whether children or adults), then, must always be seen and treated as human subjects deserving of dignity and respect, and never perceived or handled as objects of manipulation to be inserted into a struggle for power or control.

It is clear that Pope John Paul sees this catechism as one of the most critical achievements of his pontificate. Reflecting on it with the priests of the world in his 1993 Holy Thursday letter to them, he wrote, "Indeed, in this summary of the deposit of faith, we can find an authentic and sure norm for teaching Catholic doctrine, for catechetical activity among the Christian people, for that 'new evangelization' of which today's world has such immense need." He goes on to note, "In the journey toward the great jubilee of the year 2000, the Church has succeeded in producing, after the Second Vatican Council, a compendium of her teaching on faith and morality, on sacramental life and prayer. This synthesis can support our priestly ministry in various ways. It can also enlighten the apostolic awareness of our brothers and sisters who, following their Christian vocation, desire together with us to account for that hope (cf. 1 Peter 3:15) which gives us life in Jesus Christ."

The last citation makes several important observations. First, we notice the Holy Father's concern that the Church be ready for the great millennium, a readiness that implies and presupposes a thorough grasp of Catholic doctrine. Second, he seems to take aim at two extremes in the Church, both of which considered an authoritative presentation of Catholic Faith after Vatican II to be an impossibility: "Liberals," who have argued that such a project cannot be achieved and should not be achieved in the post-conciliar era of pluralism, etc.; "conservatives," who have held that the post-conciliar confusion has been so total that no one, Pope included, could ever again state what must be believed to be a Catholic. The publication of this catechism puts the lie to both assertions. Third, the Pope looks toward the involvement of priests as the primary catechists in the Church, but also the rest of Christ's faithful who will work according to their own gifts and unique vocations. Finally, he reminds all of the need to regard knowledge of Christ and life in him to be but two sides of the same coin, both absolutely indispensable and inseparable.

DISCUSSION QUESTIONS

1. Why was the *Catechism of the Catholic Church* written?

2. Although useful for all the faithful, why are bishops the catechism's primary audience?

3. In broad terms, what four sources were used in writing the catechism?

4. What are the four major sections of the catechism?

5. How are the "In Brief" summaries particularly helpful?

part one:
THE PROFESSION OF FAITH

God, our Creator and Lord, can be known
with certainty from his works, by the
natural light of human reason.
Vatican Council I

part one:
THE PROFESSION OF FAITH

With the introductory material handled, our "tour" now moves to the substance of Part One of the *Catechism of the Catholic Church*, "The Profession of Faith." This part is concerned with man's search for God, God's movement toward man in divine revelation and then the response of faith. As we embark upon our study of the Creed, it is good to understand just what a creed is and also what we mean by the word "believe."

SECTION ONE: "I BELIEVE"—"WE BELIEVE"

Every religious community in history has gathered around certain key tenets that become enshrined in a definitive text: the Greek word for such a document is *symbolon*, the meaning of which is quite instructive. *Symbolon* is derived from *syn + ballo*, which thus comes to signify putting things together in such a way as to bring about a unity. Interestingly, the opposite is *diabolos*, deriving from *dia + ballo*, to throw into confusion. Thus, a statement of faith brings about and ensures the unity of all believers, while the work of the Evil One is pre-cisely the causing of confusion, turmoil and disunity. A tan-gible profession of faith is not a straightjacket; rather it is an instrument that frees people from confusion and launches them on the road to oneness under God and among themselves.

It is sometimes disputed as to whether or not a creed should be recited in the first singular or plural. To be sure, the Latin is singular (*credo*), but the Greek original is plural (*pisteuomen*). In fact, both the singular and the plural understandings are needed for a complete picture. Personal belief is essential, and no one can believe on behalf of another; hence, the importance of the singular. On the other hand, the belief that an individual professes comes from a community of faith and is reinforced in that body. Put simply, I believe what we believe and be-cause we believe; the singular and plural are but two sides of the same coin and should not be seen in opposition but as complementary.

Man's Capacity for God

The first chapter of the catechism is devoted to "man's ca-pacity for God." Here we are reminded that "man is by nature and vocation a religious being" (44). This might come as news to those who have bought into a totally secular method of con-sidering the human person as little more than so many pounds of minerals or so many organs to be harvested. Similarly, those who have become jaundiced by modern insensibility to divin-ity may find it hard to accept the truth, firmly held by the Church, that "man lives a fully human life only if he freely lives by his bond to God" (ibid.). In other words, we Catholics still accept the wisdom and insight of St. Augustine, who con-fessed that "Thou hast made us for thyself, O Lord, and our hearts are restless until they rest in Thee."

Furthermore, unlike various types of Christians skeptical of human reason, the Catholic Church holds to the belief, so well enunciated at Vatican I, that "God, our Creator and Lord, can be known with certainty from his works, by the natural light of human reason" (47). Hence, built into the very structure of man and the universe is the fundamental ability to come to a real, though imperfect, knowledge of God: the Creator comes into focus through his creation. And although our human language is, by its very nature, necessarily limited, we can still speak of God and his perfections in ways that are adequate, even if not exhaustive, of the great mystery of God. Finally, the chapter ends with the reminder from *Gaudium et Spes* (36) that "without the Creator, the creature vanishes"—a point that should scarcely need to be made in an age so torn by strife and human destruction, all because the various ideologies of modernity (Communism, Nazism, Fascism, secularism, materialism, etc.) have sought to eliminate God from human affairs.

The Nature of Revelation

"God's search for man" provides the substance of the reflection of the next chapter. Therefore, we are not left to our own devices to unravel the mystery of God; on the contrary, God has approached us. The text goes on to delineate the ways in which that divine revelation has occurred from God's overtures to our first parents (both before and after the Fall), to Noah (as an outreach to the Gentiles), to Abraham (in establishing the covenant by which the Chosen People were formed and sustained), and finally (in every sense of that word), God's revelation and covenant in and through Jesus Christ. The catechism notes that the motivation for this divine self-disclosure, done so gradually and carefully, is nothing other than a sign of God's love (cf. 68).

How is this revelation transmitted?—through Apostolic Tradition, which is comprised of two distinct but integrally related moments. The first is "the apostolic preaching"; that is "the Gospel was handed on in two ways," orally and in writing (cf. 76). That body of doctrine is then "continued by apostolic succession." "This living transmission, accomplished by the Holy Spirit, is called Tradition," through which "the Church, in her doctrine, life, and worship perpetuates and transmits to every generation all that she herself is, all that she believes" (78). No false dichotomy here between Scripture and Tradition as we recognize that the apostolic preaching began, as the word implies, in an oral form and was then committed to writing and is now preserved and passed on through those men who stand on the shoulders of the apostles, namely, the bishops, whose task it is "faithfully [to] preserve, expound, and spread [the message] abroad by their preaching" (81). This entire process is established by God and protected by him because it is the means whereby God communicates his very Self to the human race through his Son's Church. In other words, why would God have bothered about the work of revelation if he had not safeguarded the message, thus refusing to allow every person to fend for himself or, worse yet, allow for the possibility of having people fall into error? The response of the whole Church should be gratitude to Almighty God, manifested when all the faithful "receive with docility the teachings and directives that their pastors give them in different forms" (87), once more pointing to the essential unity that should be the hallmark of Christ's Church.

Relying on the formula of Vatican II's *Dei Verbum*, the catechism teaches that Scripture and Tradition, in reality, "flowing out from the same divine well-spring, come together in some fashion to form one thing, and move towards the same goal" (80). This is encapsulated as "one common source . . . two distinct modes of transmission." It continues by making the critical distinction between "apostolic tradition," which is unchangeable since from the apostles, and "ecclesial traditions," which constitute "particular forms, adapted to different places and times, in which the great Tradition is expressed" (83).

But who may interpret this "great Tradition"? It "has been entrusted to the bishops in communion with the successor of Peter, the bishop of Rome" (85). So, can the ecclesiastical hierarchy say Tradition is whatever they want? Hardly, since the catechism immediately goes on to note, with Vatican II's *Dei Verbum,* that "this Magisterium is not superior to the Word of God, but is its servant. It teaches only what has been handed on to it" (86). This is important to understand in the context of various contemporary concerns as some suppose that it is simply stubbornness on the part of the Pope and bishops that refuses to change Church teaching on a host of issues from abortion to artificial birth control to the ordination of women. The fact of the matter is not that they do not wish to do so (which is really irrelevant), but that they *cannot* do so.

What is the role of dogmas in the life of the Church? They "are lights along the path of faith" (89), a beautiful way to express the centrality and indispensability of dogma in Catholic life. Thus, dogma is not an appendage, or, worse yet, a necessary (or even unnecessary!) evil. Instead, "there is an organic connection between our spiritual life and the dogmas" (89). Furthermore, while noting the existence of a "hierarchy of truths," the catechism observes that there is also an essential "coherence" among the various teachings, which go to make up "the whole of the Revelation of the mystery of Christ" (90). In plain English, "pick and choose Catholicism" is out of bounds. Another sign of the ongoing presence of the Holy Spirit in the Church is that, "thanks to its supernatural sense of faith, the People of God" (i.e., hierarchy, clergy and laity alike) "as a whole never ceases to welcome, to penetrate more deeply, and to live more fully from the gift of divine Revelation" (99).

Sacred Scripture

The chapter on Sacred Scripture contains a wealth of information that needs to be thoroughly digested; summaries will not do justice to the depth of insight. Nevertheless, one can cite a few more salient statements. "All Sacred Scripture is but one book, and that one book is Christ, because all divine Scripture speaks of Christ, and all divine Scripture is fulfilled in Christ" (134). This notion is the key to a proper interpretation of the Bible—one to which the early Fathers adhered most firmly and one lost in recent years. Therefore, from a Catholic perspective, every line of Scripture from Genesis to Revelation concerns the Son of God and is to be understood in the light of the Christ event, thus making a unity of "God's plan and his Revelation" (140).

Repeating Catholic teaching reaffirmed at Vatican II, the catechism reminds all of the inerrancy of the Scriptures, which "teach without error his saving truth" (136). Restated is the number of biblical books (forty-six for the Old Testament and twenty-seven for the New), with the additional note that "the four Gospels occupy a central place because Christ Jesus is their center" (139).

The Human Response to God

Chapter III concerns "man's response to God." The catechism stresses that "faith is a personal adherence of the whole man to God who reveals himself. . . . an assent of the intellect and will" (176). "To believe," then, "has thus a twofold reference: to the person and to the truth; to the truth, by trust in the person who bears witness to it." Once again we discover the elimination of false dichotomies that would have people ask whether their faith should rest in God or in doctrines. One believes the truths of faith because they are revealed by "no one but God; the Father, the Son, and the Holy Spirit" (cf. 177-78). Realizing that faith is a work of God and not man, we are taught that "man needs the interior helps of the Holy Spirit" for it (179).

Attempting to probe the depths of faith, the catechism says that "'believing' is a human act, conscious and free, corresponding to the dignity of the human person" (180); therefore, it cannot be forced if both the act and the person are to be held in honor. At the same time, the act of faith is "an ecclesial act" (181). This goes back to the delicate interplay discussed earlier between the "I" and the "we" in professing the faith, which action "is necessary for salvation" (183), and which is also "a foretaste of the knowledge that will make us blessed in the life to come" (184).

The Nature of Creeds

The standard profession of faith expounded in catechisms is the so-called Apostles' Creed, the most primitive and the one that a pious legend holds was created when each of the Twelve Apostles contributed one article each. This creed is divided into three major parts, dealing with the Father, the Son and the Holy Spirit; significantly, the Church is considered under the Holy Spirit since she draws her life and meaning from the one whom the Nicene Creed (the next most popular) calls "the Lord and Giver of life." Creeds have been formulated by councils (e.g., Nicea, Toledo, Trent) and by popes (e.g., the 1968 "Credo of the People of God" by Pope Paul VI). They are usually an attempt to deal with certain points especially controverted at a particular period of history or to solidify "the faith which comes to us from the apostles" (Roman Canon). For which reason the catechism asserts that "to say the Credo with faith is to enter into communion with God, Father, Son, and Holy Spirit, and also with the whole Church which transmits the faith to us and in whose midst we believe" (197).

SECTION TWO:
THE PROFESSION OF THE CHRISTIAN FAITH

God the Father Almighty

In this section we read that "the Credo begins with God the Father, for the Father is the first divine person of the Most Holy Trinity; our Creed begins with the creation of heaven and earth, for creation is the beginning and foundation of all God's works" (198). A good explanation is offered of the primacy of the Godhead, who is one or unique, as well as the progressive nature of God's self-disclosure to the human race. Noting a major development in that process, the catechism cites God's communication to the people of Israel of his sacred Name, which "expresses a person's essence and identity and the meaning of this person's life" (203). The Name also reminds us that God "is not an anonymous force" (203). Furthermore, the Name revealed to Moses (Yahweh) "is mysterious just as God is mystery. It is at once a name revealed and something like the refusal of a name," thus demonstrating how God is "the hidden God," whose "name is ineffable" (206). In this connection, a quotation from St. Augustine is made: "If you comprehended Him, He wouldn't be God" (201). And yet, he is also the one who "is always there, present to his people" (207).

A salutary reminder is offered: "Believing in God, the only One, and loving him with all our being has enormous consequences for our whole life." Those consequences are then delineated: "It means coming to know God's greatness and majesty . . . living in thanksgiving. . . . knowing the unity and true dignity of all men. . . . making good use of created things. . . . trusting God in every circumstance" (222-27). Giving still further elucidation to the Divine Name, the catechism teaches: "The God of our faith has revealed himself as He who is: and he has made himself known as 'abounding in steadfast love and faithfulness' (Ex 34:6). God's very being is Truth and Love" (231).

An excellent history and analysis of Trinitarian doctrine is given, underscoring the foundational nature of this truth of faith, "the source of all the other mysteries of faith" (234). This doctrine cannot be overstressed since most Catholics probably live their lives blissfully ignorant of the meaning of the Trinity, let alone the implications of the doctrine for their daily experience. The "In Brief" section here is a goldmine of insights into this basic doctrine.

For example, "God alone can make it known to us by revealing himself as Father, Son, and Holy Spirit" (261). "The Incarnation of God's Son reveals that God is the eternal Father and that the Son is consubstantial with the Father, which means that, in the Father and with the Father, the Son is one and the same God" (262); "The mission of the Holy Spirit, sent by the Father in the name of the Son and by the Son . . . reveals that, with them, the Spirit is one and the same God" (263); "The Holy Spirit proceeds from the Father as the first principle and, by the eternal gift of this to the Son, from the communion of both the Father and the Son" (264); through the grace of Baptism in the name of the Trinity, "we are called to share in the life of the Blessed Trinity, here on earth in the obscurity of faith, and after death in eternal light" (265).

The statement on the procession of the Holy Spirit appears to have been carefully crafted as an opening to the Eastern Orthodox, so as to handle the thorny, but not insurmountable, problem of how the Churches of East and West present this truth. Quoting the Athanasian Creed, the catechism recalls for us that the Godhead is one, "Their glory equal, their majesty coeternal" (266). And then making a critical point the text says, "Inseparable in what they are, the divine persons are also inseparable in what they do" (267). In other words, although we assign certain "tasks" to particular Persons (e.g., creation to the Father), the Triune God is active in all such works, for where one Person is present, all are present.

Next follows a fine exposition on the omnipotence of God that urges us to make our own the prayer of Job: "I know that you can do all things, and that no purpose of yours can be thwarted (42:2)" (275). Establishing the linkage between liturgy and doctrine, the catechism (276) observes how often the prayer of the Church calls on the Lord as "*omnipotens sempiterne Deus*" (almighty and eternal God), a line generally eliminated from the English version of the collects in the 1970s, because some said it made God seem too distant, replacing it with "Father," which now has come under fire from feminists! In a touching reflection we are led to consider that "God shows forth his almighty power by converting us from our sins and restoring us to his friendship by grace" (277); thus, God is never more powerful than in his mercy.

Creation

The section on creation is masterfully done, giving due play to science, all the while stressing the irreplaceable and indispensable role of a loving and providential Creator-God. To demonstrate the essential compatibility of religion and science,

Solomon's thoughts are brought forward as worth pondering: "For He gave me sound knowledge of existing things, that I might know the organization of the universe and the force of its elements, the beginning and the end and the midpoint of times, the changes in the sun's course and the variations of the seasons . . ." (Wis 7:17-21). A summary of the Christian doctrine of creation highlights the following teachings: "In the creation of the world and of man, God gave the first and universal witness to his almighty love and his wisdom, the first proclamation of the 'plan of his loving goodness,' which finds its goal in the new creation in Christ" (315), thus grounding God's creative activity in the Christ-event. Returning to an earlier theme, we are made to remember that "though the work of creation is attributed to the Father in particular, it is equally a truth of faith that the Father, Son, and Holy Spirit together are the one, indivisible principle of creation" (316). Furthermore, "God alone created the universe freely, directly, and without any help" (317), that creation occurred "'out of nothing'" unlike what any other creature can ever accomplish (318). Spelling out the divine rationale for creation, the catechism states that this was done by God "to show forth and communicate his glory. That his creatures should share in his truth, goodness, and beauty — this is the glory for which God created them" (319); hence, this is not a deity possessed of megalomania but of incredible depths of love, desirous of sharing the deepest and most wonderful aspects of himself with those he loved from all eternity. The text is careful to observe that "God created the universe and keeps it in existence by his Word," Jesus Christ, "and by his Creator Spirit, the giver of life," once more emphasizing the Trinitarian dimension of creation, as well as the importance of belief in divine providence that is also presented as guiding "all his creatures with wisdom and love to their ultimate end" (320-21). This "filial trust in the providence of our heavenly Father" is seen as a special teaching of Christ; likewise, it is evident in God's giving to human beings the ability "to cooperate freely with his plans" (322-23). Taking on the question of evil, the catechism asserts that "the fact that God permits physical and even moral evil is a mystery that God illuminates by his Son Jesus Christ who died and rose to vanquish evil. Faith gives us the certainty that God would not permit an evil if he did not cause a good to come from that very evil, by ways that we shall fully know only in eternal life" (324).

In dealing with belief in divine providence and with the problem of evil, the catechism is certainly addressing issues of critical importance to generations that have beheld some of the most horrifying examples of evil in history, as we are brought to evaluate all these occurrences in the light of revelation and Christian faith—something all too often neglected in Christian teaching, preaching and counselling.

The catechism next turns its attention to the creation of "heaven and earth," of that which is "seen and unseen" (325). The English translation of the Nicene Creed once more obfuscates a truth of faith as we speak of what is "seen and unseen," a focus somewhat different from the Greek and Latin originals since "invisible" is not a synonym for "unseen" (which can indeed become visible, for instance, if someone is merely hiding temporarily). This is not pedantry because it undergirds faith in spiritual (as opposed to material) aspects of created reality. The first result of that is acceptance of the doctrine of angels, which is termed "a truth of faith" (328); angels "are servants and messengers of God" (329). "As purely *spiritual* creatures angels have intelligence and will," creatures with individual personality and immortality (329-30). The place of angels is also connected to the life of Christ and the life of the Church that professes her faith in these beings in the daily liturgy and in the observance of their feasts. St. Basil is used to teach that "beside each believer stands an angel as protector and shepherd leading him to life" (331-36). These are among many of the lost or forgotten catechetical truths of the post-conciliar period, now restated with clarity and with great potential for our life in Christ.

"The Visible World" opens with the solemn declaration that "nothing exists that does not owe its existence to God the Creator. The world began when God's word drew it out of nothingness; . . . [the] primordial event" (338). The instruction then comes that "each creature possesses its own particular goodness and perfection," which realization requires that "man must therefore respect the particular goodness of every creature, to avoid any disordered use of things," resulting in scorn for the Creator and disaster for man and his environment (339). Many other conclusions flow from all this: the interdependence of creatures; the beauty of the universe; the hierarchy of creatures; man as the peak of creation; solidarity among all creatures (340-44). Two other less-noted insights are mentioned, too. First is the role of the Sabbath, in view of which "creation was fashioned," thus leading us to "the worship and adoration of God" (347). Second is the notion of the "eighth day. . . . the day of Christ's Resurrection . . . [which] begins the new creation. Thus, the work of creation culminates in the greater work of redemption . . . the new creation in Christ, the splendor of which surpasses that of the first creation" (349).

Man: The Image of God

Much is made of the creation of man in God's own image, and rightly so. Therefore, "only man is 'able to know and love his creator'. . . [and] is 'the only creature on earth that God has willed for its own sake,' and he alone is called to share. . . in God's own life." Indeed this is the very end and "fundamental reason for his dignity" (356), a dignity that calls one, "by grace, to a covenant with his Creator" (357). Then comes the emphasis on the human person as "a being at once corporeal and spiritual," with the understanding, then, that "man, whole and entire, is therefore willed by God," thus avoiding a crass materialism that would deny or avoid discussions of the immaterial but also an equally deleterious spiritualization of man, such that Plato's notion of "the soul to be the 'form' of the body" could take hold in Christian thought (362). The catechism explains in great detail the Church's understanding of the word "soul," which "signifies the spiritual principle in man" (363). To avoid an unhealthy dualism, the text says that "the human body shares in the dignity of 'the image of God'; it is a human body precisely because it is animated by a spiritual soul, and it is the whole human person that is intended to become, in the Body of Christ, a temple of the Spirit" (364). Answering questions raised by various scientific theories, another paragraph speaks of the soul as being "created immediately by God" and, furthermore, that this soul "will be reunited with the body at the final Resurrection" (366).

Much attention is paid to the matter of the creation of man and woman, especially as regards their basic "equality and difference willed by God" (369). Engaging in very careful exegesis of Genesis, the catechism stresses that man and woman were "created together," part of the reason for the equality (371). The unmistakable imprint of Pope John Paul II is found particularly in this section, as it teaches that God "created [man and woman] to be a communion of persons" (372); no precis like this can even seek to do justice to the profundity of the teaching offered, thoroughly rooted in Scripture and Tradition.

The text then moves on to speak of this original couple, quoting Trent as "constituted in an original 'state of holiness and justice,' [that] was 'to share in . . . divine life'" (375). This statement, of course, becomes the point of departure for the treatment of the Fall. In answer to those who have thought and taught otherwise of late, the catechism refers to "original sin [as] an essential truth of the faith" (388). While acknowledging that "the account of the Fall . . . uses figurative language," there is nonetheless an affirmation of it as "a primeval event, a deed that took place at the beginning of the history of man" (390).

Original Sin

"Revelation gives us the certainty of faith that the whole of human history is marked by the original fault freely committed by our first parents" (390). This fall of man, connected to the fall of the angels, implicates all human beings (402); hence, the necessity of Baptism "for the remission of sins [given] even [to] tiny infants who have not committed personal sin," for this original sin is "contracted" by us and "not committed"; it is "a state and not an act" (403-04). Catholics, however, are not Lutheran; therefore, we believe that although we are deprived of "original holiness and justice . . . human nature has not been totally corrupted." The effects of original sin are seen especially in that human nature "is wounded in the natural powers proper to it; subject to ignorance, suffering, and the dominion of death; and inclined to sin (concupiscence)." What has Baptism to do with all this? It gives "the life of Christ's grace, erases original sin and turns a man back toward God, but the consequences for nature, weakened and inclined to evil, persist in man and summon him to spiritual battle" (405). The tone of the statement is not at all pessimistic, but it is certainly imbued with realism.

Optimism ends up occupying center stage as the chapter ends with a discussion of the promise of a Redeemer in the Protoevangelium (or first proclamation of the Gospel) in Genesis 3:15, as well as in the mention of Mary as the New Eve "who benefited first of all and uniquely from Christ's victory over sin" (410-11). Christians, then, are not unduly weighed down by sin; in fact, they can join the chant of the lovely Exsultet which sings of the "happy fault, which gained for us so great a Redeemer!" (412), to whom our attention is directed in the next major section.

God's Only Son

The heart of the Gospel message, according to the second chapter of this section, is that God has sent his Son. Therefore, at the heart of all catechesis is the goal set forth by Pope John Paul II in *Catechesi Tradendae* and adopted by the catechism: "[To place] 'people in communion . . . with Jesus Christ: only he can lead us to the love of the Father in the Spirit and make us share in the life of the Holy Trinity'" (426). Which is to say that the overriding purpose of catechesis is transcendental, a point highlighted by the catechism's frequent reliance on "mystery" to describe events in the life of Christ to be considered.

The first event, in every way, is his Incarnation. We are invited to reflect on the names and titles of the Second Person of the Blessed Trinity. Jesus tells us of his "will [to] to save his people from their sins" (452). With no embarrassment and even less false ecumenism, the text goes on to underscore the insight of the apostolic community, namely, that there is no other name given to men by which we can be saved (cf. Acts 4:12). Next comes his title (not name) of "Christ" or "Messiah," which links him to the Chosen People as "the object of [their] hope"

(453). While acknowledging that the expression "son of God" had a variety of meanings, the catechism explains that very soon the followers of Jesus understood that this term had a particularity about it when referring to their Master. It "signifies the unique and eternal relation of Jesus Christ to God his Father: he is the only Son of the Father; he is God himself" (454). To stave off any possible confusion, it is clearly and immediately stated that "to be a Christian, one must believe that Jesus Christ is the Son of God" (454).

Next, we are treated to an excellent historical review of the title "Lord" as used in the Hebrew Scriptures and subsequently applied to Jesus in the New Testament, culminating in its use as the Church's title of choice for Jesus in the liturgy from earliest times (cf. "Maranatha" in the Book of Revelation) to the present (e.g., "The LORD be with you" ". . . through Christ our LORD"). "The title 'Lord' indicates the divine sovereignty. To confess or invoke Jesus as Lord is to believe in his divinity" (455).

The Mystery of the Incarnation

The Creed moves on to consider precisely the Incarnation: The Son of God became man. Four reasons are offered for this event: to save us in reconciling us with God (457); that we might thus know personally the love of God (458); that the Word might be our model of sanctity (459); to render us sharers in the divine nature (460). What a wealth of material for personal prayer and meditation, let alone for teaching and preaching about this doctrine, which is "the distinctive sign of Christian faith" (463). But this essential element of Christianity did not emerge full-blown from the brow of Zeus; it required much study and debate, much openness to the Holy Spirit whom Christ had promised to his apostles to lead them into all truth (cf. Jn 16: 13). In point of fact, one could almost say that the various Christological heresies were needed to bring about the necessary clarification and precision; hence, a fine review of those aberrant teachings is also given. As one moves through the list, one is convinced of the truth of Fulton Sheen's insight that today we are merely confronted by "old heresies with new labels."

A good discussion follows on the humanity of Christ—his soul, knowledge, will and body. His sacred humanity is epitomized in his love for us by means of "a human heart" (478), and thus so worthy of our love and devotion in return.

Key doctrinal points conclude the section (479-83): "The eternal Word . . . became incarnate; without losing his divine nature he has assumed a human nature." "Jesus Christ is true God and true man, in the unity of his divine person; for this reason he is the one and only mediator between God and men." He "possesses two natures, one divine and the other human, not confused, but united in the one person of God's Son." And so, he "has a human intellect and will, perfectly attuned and subject to his divine intellect and divine will, which he has in common with the Father and the Holy Spirit." All this, then, is the mystery of the Incarnation, that "wonderful union" of the two natures in the one Person of the Word.

The Virginal Conception and Birth

What does the Creed mean when speaking of the Lord's conception by the Holy Spirit and his birth from the Virgin Mary? This doctrine emphasizes the primacy of the divine action in the human life of the Son of God, from its very beginning, as the Holy Spirit "sanctif[ied] the womb of the Virgin Mary" and made it fruitful through His divine power (485). Then comes a superb presentation on the place of Mary in the plan of salvation, with the observation that "what the Catholic Faith believes about Mary is based on what it believes about Christ, and what it teaches about Mary illumines, in turn, its faith in Christ" (487). This connection between Christ and Mary is critical and is obviously grounded in the will of God himself, for the humanity of the Son of God was the very one drawn from hers (481). Mariological issues presented include: the predestination of Mary; her Immaculate Conception; her obedience, faith and divine maternity; Mary's perpetual virginity. The doctrinal capsules given teach that: "From the first instant of her conception, she was totally preserved from the stain of original sin and she remained pure from all personal sin throughout her life" (508); it is right to call her "Mother of God" for a Christological reason, "[because] she is the mother of the eternal Son of God made man, who is God himself (509); in the words of St. Thomas Aquinas, we are reminded that Mary "uttered her yes [to God] 'in the name of all human nature'" (511).

Demonstrating how catechesis is tied to prayer and spirituality, the catechism deals with the mysteries of the life of Christ, so that one sees the truth of the assertion of *Catechesi Tradendae*: "The whole of Christ's life was a continual teaching'" in every aspect (561). This is so because "Christ's disciples are to conform themselves to him until he is formed in them. 'For this reason we, who have been made like to him,who have died with him and risen with him, are taken up into the mysteries of his life, until we reign together with him'" (562). Let one lovely example of this type of application suffice: "Shepherd or wiseman, [no one] can approach God here below except by kneeling before the manger at Bethlehem and adoring him hidden in the weakness of a new-born child" (563).

Tackling Some Knotty Problems

Since even a cursory reading of the Gospels reveals that the Kingdom of God was the focus of the preaching, teaching and miracles of Jesus, due consideration is given to that reality. The somewhat vexing question of the relation of Church and Kingdom is handled carefully and ably. Are Kingdom and Church two completely separate entities? Do they admit of total identification between them? We learn that "the Church is the seed and beginning of this kingdom." Therefore, neither full identification nor disjunction is a correct explanation. Simply put, the Kingdom that Jesus inaugurated during his earthly life and ministry but which would not blossom in all its glory until the Lord comes again, can be found in seed in the Church Christ established. Furthermore, the catechism reminds all that the "keys [of that kingdom] are entrusted to Peter" (567), and by extension, to his successors.

Before launching into a treatment of the passion and death of Christ, the catechism stresses that circumstances of these events were "faithfully handed on by the Gospels" (573). While this would seem self-evident to the average believer, it is unfortately not uncommon that certain members of the scholarly world have debated this matter and even rejected the point here taught.

The relationship between Jesus and Judaism is presented in a manner that is fair, honest and sensitive, always careful to speak of "certain Jews" (594), rather than the whole nation, since the Scriptures demonstrates that, in reality, Jesus was a point of division among Jewish authorities (593), very importantly, that "neither all Jews indiscriminately at that time, nor Jews today, can be charged with the crimes committed during his Passion" (597), emphasizing a traditional teaching of Christian faith and spirituality, that all "sinners were the authors and the ministers of all the sufferings that the divine Redeemer endured" (598). Equally valuable to understand is the fact that this death was not the result of happenstance or misfortune; on the contrary, it belongs to "the mystery of God" (599) and was thus willed by him. The text goes on to teach, with St. Paul, that "God 'made [Christ] to be sin'" for us (602) and out of a love that "is not restrictive," for Jesus died "for all men without exception" (605). Perhaps this will help quell the disturbance of some who argue that the consecratory formula of the Mass in English should not speak of Christ's blood being shed "for all" but merely "for many."

The Lord's Death and Burial

But this death of Christ was not imposed on him; he freely took it upon himself out of love for man (609). Because of its centrality, he wished his disciples to remember him and it until the end of time. Therefore, "the Eucharist that Christ institutes at [the Last Supper] will be the memorial of his sacrifice." Lest anyone not understand how this sacrifice can continue in the Church, the catechism declares that it happens because "the Lord institut[ed] his apostles as priests of the New Covenant" (611). In this "unique and definitive sacrifice" (613) . . . "Jesus substitutes his obedience for our disobedience" (615). The whole section is summarized in the thought of St. Rose of Lima: "Apart from the cross, there is no other ladder by which we may get to heaven" (618). Once again, doctrine and the spiritual life reinforce one another.

What is the value of the Creed's insistence on the burial of Christ? It highlights the reality of his death: "To the benefit of every man, Jesus Christ tasted death. It is truly the Son of God made man who died and was buried" (629). It also prefigures our own burial with Christ in Baptism, whereby the merits of his saving death and Resurrection provide us with a new life (628). Another seemingly esoteric article of the Creed refers to his "[descent] into hell." Once more, we are told that this line gives expression to the reality of the Lord's death for us, by which "[he] conquered death and the devil" (636). Furthermore, "the dead Christ went down to the realm of the dead. He opened heaven's gates for the just who had gone before him" (637).

The Resurrection and Ascension

Exposition of the Resurrection comes next, with its characteristics as equally "the historical and transcendent event" (639), which is to say that it is something that really and truly happened in time and space but also, because it is an act of God, one which transcends human categories and limitations. Until the time of the Enlightenment, anyone who contested the veracity of the Resurrection simply left Christianity; since then, however, many have chosen to stay and either ignore, reinterpret or deny this central dogma of faith. For all these reasons, the catechism devotes much space to the Resurrection of Christ, "an essential sign" of which was the empty tomb (640). The text examines the various appearances of the Risen Christ. Again responding to contemporary concerns, the catechism takes on some recent theories and dismisses them: "Therefore the hypothesis that the Resurrection was produced by the apostles' faith [or credulity] will not hold up. On the contrary their faith in the Resurrection was born, under the action of divine grace, from their direct experience of the reality of the risen Jesus" (644). So much for the famous comment that finding the body of Jesus in a tomb today would do nothing to harm one's Christian faith!

Reviewing the continuity between Jesus' earthly and risen existence, the text cites his ability to be touched and to eat a meal, as well as to bear the marks of his saving death. At the same time, the risen Christ possessed "a glorious body" not bound by space and time, making him "[enjoy] the sovereign freedom of appearing as he wishes " (645). And so, it should be clear that we are not beholding in this event "a return to earthly life," like the other resurrections Jesus worked before his own; all those raised by him had to resume their normal lives and die again. That was not the case for him, whose Resurrection made him "[share] the divine life in his glorious state" (646).

The Resurrection of Jesus is a "work of the Holy Trinity." In other words, the entire Godhead was operative in this "transcendent intervention of God himself in creation and history" (648). This theology assists in coming to grips with the fact that one can say that Jesus raised himself from the dead and that he was raised by the power of the Father and the work of the Holy Spirit. But what did the Resurrection accomplish? First, it "is the fulfillment of the promises both of the Old Testament and of Jesus himself during his earthly life" (652). Second, "the truth of Jesus' divinity is confirmed by his Resurrection" (653). Third, by it, Christ "opens for us the way to a new life. . . . reinstat[ing] us in God's grace," which is nothing less than "filial adoption," enabling us to become brothers and sisters of Christ. It is important to say, however, that this identity is not ours "by nature, but by the gift of grace" (654). "Finally," says the catechism, " Christ's Resurrection—and the risen Christ himself—is the principle and source of our future resurrection" (655).

The sixth article of the Creed is concerned with the ascension of the Lord and his being seated at the Father's right hand. It is possible to believe all this, without its having any effect in or on one's life in Christ. This would indeed be tragic. Therefore, the catechism spells out some of the meaning in three points: The ascension of Christ marks the definitive entrance of the humanity of Jesus into the heavenly domain of God, whence he shall return, but that heavenly realm in the meantime conceals him from the eyes of men (655). "Jesus Christ, the head of the Church, precedes us into the Father's glorious kingdom so that we, the members of his Body, may live in the hope of one day being with him forever" (666). "Jesus Christ, having entered the sanctuary of heaven once and for all, intercedes constantly for us as the mediator who assures us of the permanent outpouring of the Holy Spirit" (667). No dead doctrines here, but ones that give substance to life now and in the hereafter.

The Parousia and Last Judgement

Christ "will come again in glory," we pray. But how does he exercise his kingship until then? "Through the Church" (668): "[having] fully accomplished his mission, Christ dwells on earth in his Church" (669), picking up the theme touched on earlier. No surprise, then, that "'the Church on earth is endowed already with a sanctity that is real but imperfect'" (670). (This, in spite of translators of the Mass into English who have dropped "holy" from the attributes of the Church, which the prayer, *Orate Fratres*, calls "his *holy* Church.") At the same time, one must realize that "already present in his Church, Christ's reign is nevertheless yet to be fulfilled 'with power and great glory'" (671). Indeed, this incipient Kingdom, which is the Church, is assailed "by evil powers." That is why the Church never ceases to beseech Christ with the words: "Come, Lord Jesus," for only he can endow his bride with the robe of glory. Very wisely, the catechism recalls that the present moment is not the hour of "the definitive order of justice, love, and peace. According to the Lord, the present time is the time of the Spirit and of witness, but also a time still marked by 'distress' and the trial of evil which does not spare the Church and ushers in the struggles of the last days. It is a time of waiting and watching" (672). How true that is can be seen by the treatment received by the Church in these present times.

The text also affirms that the coming of the glorious Messiah is being delayed, pending the "recognition by 'all Israel'" of Jesus as such (674). Continuing to look toward the future, we see the final test of the Church. While holding to a real trial, the catechism urges us to reject any "falsification of the kingdom to come under the name of millenarianism, especially the 'intrinsically perverse' political form of a secular messianism" (676).

"God's triumph over the revolt of evil will take the form of the Last Judgment" (677), which task belongs to Christ, due to his being the Redeemer of the world; "He 'acquired' this right by His cross." Immediately, we are made to remember, however, that "the Son did not come to judge, but to save." How does condemnation occur then? "By rejecting grace in this life, one already judges oneself, receives according to one's works, and can even condemn oneself for all eternity by rejecting the Spirit of love" (679). Dignity and responsibility are thus stressed, enabling us and even causing us to participate in our own salvation.

THE HOLY SPIRIT

It is often alleged that Western Christianity has a very poorly developed pneumatology or theology of the Holy Spirit. The fact that the new catechism deals with the Spirit in thirteen short pages could be brought forth as evidence to substantiate the charge, however, that would be but a most superficial reading of the work. In point of fact, the Holy Spirit is not relegated to a brief tract presented in isolation but is present on nearly every page. The special focus of this section, however, is an attempt to understand what it means "to believe in the Holy Spirit . . . consubstantial with the Father and the Son: 'with the Father and the Son he is worshipped and glorified'" (685). We are reminded that it is especially in these "end times," that is, in the time between the Incarnation and the Lord's Second Coming, that the Spirit is "revealed and given, recognized and welcomed as a person" (686).

But where does this happen? Preeminently in the Church which "is the place where we know the Holy Spirit" and in a multiplicity of ways: in the Scriptures, the Tradition, the Magisterium; in the sacramental liturgy and prayer; "in the charisms and ministries by which the Church is built up; in the signs of apostolic and missionary life; in the witness of saints through whom he manifests his holiness and continues the work of salvation" (688). It is no accident, then, that the article of the Creed concerned with the Church follows immediately the one on the Holy Spirit.

Moving on to a consideration of the inner life of the Holy Spirit within the Blessed Trinity, the catechism recalls that the Three Persons "are distinct but inseparable" (689). His proper name is "Holy Spirit," given to him by Christ himself and used by the Church in Baptism. It goes on to explain that this title is a rendering of the Hebrew word "*ruah*, which, in its primary sense, means breath, air, wind" and which was used by the Lord Himself to teach Nicodemus about the One Who "is personally God's breath, the divine Spirit." Continuing on, we discover that while "'Spirit' and 'Holy' are divine attributes common to the three divine persons," both Sacred Scripture and theological language apply the two words together in a manner uniquely appropriate to the Holy Spirit (691). We are then treated to a listing of the various names of the Holy Spirit found in Sacred Scripture: Paraclete, Spirit of truth, Spirit of promise, Spirit of adoption, Spirit of Christ, Spirit of the Lord, Spirit of God, the Spirit of glory.

Signs and Symbols of the Holy Spirit

As rich as the nomenclature is, so is the variety of symbols for the Spirit found in Christian iconography to depict the ways in which the Spirit and his life are manifested in the Church and in the world. These are *Water*, which "becomes the efficacious sacramental sign of new birth" (694); *Anointing*, so much so that in the Johannine literature the Spirit and the anointing are synonymous; beyond that, the name of Jesus as "the Christ" means precisely "the one 'anointed' by God's Spirit" (from the Hebrew 'Messiah') and, similarly, in the Eastern Churches the rite of Confirmation is called "chrismation"—all pointing to the direct work of the anointing of the Holy Spirit (695); *Fire*, which "symbolizes the transforming energy of the Holy Spirit's actions," that same fire which Jesus said he had come to cast upon the earth and which came to rest upon the infant Church on Pentecost, the very same fire that Paul urged the Thessalonians not to extinguish—for it is none other than the Holy Spirit himself (696).

Other symbols of the Holy Spirit include *Cloud and Light*, found in the theophanies of the Old Testament and reappearing in the New (697); *The Seal*, used in ancient times as the *sphragis* identifying a soldier as a member of a particular company or battalion, which then came into Christian theology to speak about the "seal" or "indelible character" given one touched by the Spirit of God in the three unrepeatable sacraments—Baptism, Confirmation and Holy Orders (698); *The Hand*, the imposition of which brought healing and forgiveness in both Covenants, continuing to do so in the Church's liturgy even today as the Spirit is invoked to perform his work of sanctification in the members of Christ's Body (699): *The Finger*, by which Jesus cast out demons and also the title for the Spirit in the magnificent *Veni Creator* as we call upon him as *digitus dextrae Patris*, "finger of the Father's right hand," or the personal dynamism by which God works in the world and in the hearts of men (700); and finally *The Dove*, first significant after the Flood as a testimony to the earth's inhabitability once again. Similarly, the Dove becomes prominent after the Baptism of the Lord, resting on him and dwelling with him and in all baptized in his Name (701).

The Spirit in Promise and Fulfillment

The catechism next reflects on "God's Spirit and Word in the Time of Promises," so that both Son and Spirit form part of the preparation of the Chosen People—albeit in veiled signs and symbols, awaiting the full revelation in the Person of the Incarnate Word (702). Such preparatory events were the many theophanies and, as well, the giving of the Law as during the time of the Kingdom and the Exile (705-10). The period of waiting reaches a high point in the Book of Emmanuel, the prophecies concerning the advent of the Messiah and in the Songs of the Suffering Servant who, "taking our death upon himself . . . can communicate to us his own Spirit of life" (713). For this reason, we are told, "Christ inaugurates the proclamation of the Good News by making his own the following passage from Isaiah: 'The Spirit of the Lord is upon me . . .'" (714). Likewise, part of this remote preparation for the coming of the Messiah, the One anointed by God's Spirit, was the setting aside of the *anawim*, those poor people of God who were content to wait for the Lord's establishment of justice and right; it would be they through whom the Spirit would work to prepare for the Lord a people well disposed (716).

John the Baptist was one of those *anawim;* the finest example, however, was the Blessed Virgin Mary—the highwater point in God's proximate preparation for the sending of his divine Son. In theological precision but also in near-poetic fashion, we read, "Mary, the all-holy ever-virgin Mother of God is the masterwork of the mission of the Son and the Spirit in the fullness of time. For the first time in the plan of salvation and because his Spirit had prepared her, the Father found the *dwelling place* where his Son and his Spirit could dwell among men." Rightly, then, does the liturgy refer to Mary as the "Seat of Wisdom." By way of anticipation, the catechism notes that in Mary are begun the "'wonders of God' that the Spirit was to fulfill in Christ and the Church" (721).

How did this happen in Mary? She who was "full of grace" was conceived without sin "by sheer grace" as the Spirit readied her for her sacred mission (722). "In Mary, the Holy Spirit *fulfills* the plan of the Father's loving goodness," her fruitful virginity being a special sign of the Spirit's power and of her faith. "In Mary, the Holy Spirit *manifests* the Son of the Father, now become the Son of the Virgin . . . Finally, through Mary, the Holy Spirit begins to bring men, the objects of God's merciful love, *into communion* with Christ." And then in her role as the New Eve, she becomes the Mother of what St. Augustine terms "the 'whole Christ'" (that is, his Church), as she sits in prayer in their midst awaiting the Pentecost gift of the Spirit (723-26).

The full revelation of the person and mission of the Spirit occurs in and through Jesus Christ, but only after his saving death and Resurrection; prior to that, hints are given to the multitudes and more open manifestations are made to the inner circle of disciples. At the hour of the Lord's glorification, he promises the coming of the Spirit of truth who "will be with us for ever; he will remain with us. The Spirit will teach us everything, remind us of all that Christ said to us and bear witness to him. The Holy Spirit will lead us into all truth and will glorify Christ. He will prove the world wrong about sin, righteousness, and judgment" (727-29). After his Resurrection, our Blessed Lord communicates the Holy Spirit to His disciples by breathing on them. "From this hour onward, the mission of Christ and the Spirit becomes the mission of the Church: 'As the Father has sent me, even so I send you'" (730). Once more, we see how the work of Son, Spirit and Church are conjoined and, in fact, inseparable.

The Spirit in the Church

In the coming of the Spirit and in his on-going advents in the Church's life, most especially through the sacred liturgy, the Kingdom becomes a present even if incomplete reality. The Eastern liturgy is thus quoted as demonstrating an awareness of this incipient and real presence of eternity in time: "We have seen the true Light, we have received the heavenly Spirit, we have found the true Faith: we adore the indivisible Trinity, who has saved us" (732). "The first effect" of the communication of the Spirit is "the forgiveness of our sins. The communion of the Holy Spirit in the Church restores to the baptized the divine likeness lost through sin." Worth noting is the citation of 2 Cor 13:13, the greeting at Mass so limply translated into English as *the fellowship of the Holy Spirit* but so much more powerfully evocative when seen as "the communion of the Holy Spirit"—giving to believers a share in the inner life of the Triune God (734). What, then, does the Holy Spirit *do*? "[He] *prepares* men . . . [He] *manifests* the risen Lord to them . . . [He] *makes present* the mystery of Christ, supremely in the Eucharist, in order to reconcile them, to *bring them into communion* with God, that they may 'bear much fruit'" (737). Very carefully, however, the catechism instructs us that "the Church's mission is not an addition to that of Christ and the Holy Spirit, but is its sacrament: in her whole being and in all her members, the Church is sent to announce, bear witness, make present, and spread the mystery of the communion of the Holy Trinity" (738).

In summary fashion, we are then shown how the Spirit is related to every other aspect of the Christian mystery. "Through the Church's sacraments, Christ communicates his Holy and sanctifying Spirit to the members of his Body" (739). (This will be the topic of Part Two of the catechism.) "These 'mighty works of God,' offered to believers in the sacraments of the Church, bear their fruit in the new life in Christ, according to the Spirit." (This will be the topic of Part Three.) "The Holy Spirit, the artisan of God's works, is the master of prayer" (740-41). (This will be the topic of Part Four.) Neatly tied together, then, we find the entire Christian life enlivened by the Holy Spirit, whom the Nicene Creed and Pope John Paul II's encyclical *Dominum et Vivificantem* rightly call "the Lord and Giver of life."

THE HOLY CATHOLIC CHURCH

To condense forty-five pages of text into a brief sub-chapter of a book is a frustrating exercise, especially when the topic is the meaning of life in the Church. The approach here, then, is not so much to summarize as to highlight special points of interest and/or items that have been ignored or contested in recent years.

The very title of this article of Section Two, "I Believe in the Holy Catholic Church," is important but elusive in English.

Both Latin and French distinguish between believing *in* something or someone and believing something or someone. The Creed says, "*Credo in unum Deum Patrem omnipotentem . . . in Filium . . . in Spiritum Sanctum,*" but (*credo*) "*ecclesiam,*" without the preposition. What is the significance? Very simply that one does not believe in the Church in the same way as one believes in the Trinity; I believe *in* God while I believe the Church. Or better perhaps, I believe the Church because I believe in God. The act of faith in regard to the Church is secondary to that in regard to God.

In quick fashion, the basics of ecclesiology are rehearsed, giving the etymology of "church" (the assembly) and its identity (the People of God nourished by the Body of Christ, so as to become themselves the Body of Christ). We are reminded that the Church existed as part of God's saving plan from all eternity—prepared for in the Ancient Covenant, "founded by the words and actions of Jesus Christ, fulfilled by his redeeming cross and his Resurrection," but yet to be revealed in all its glory at the end of time (778). Picking up a critical theme from Vatican II, the catechism recalls that "the Church is both visible and spiritual, a hierarchical society and the Mystical Body of Christ" (779); in other words, it is neither desirable nor possible to separate the institutional elements of the Church from the more spiritual ones. Nor is it correct to pit official Catholicism against the Catholicism of various dissenting individuals or groups.

The next section discusses the Church as the People of God, the Body of Christ and the Temple of the Holy Spirit. Again echoing Vatican II's *Lumen Gentium*, the catechism teaches that these images of the Church are not mutually exclusive but complementary. Hence, it is not legitimate to campaign under one banner in such a way as to put aside truths contained in other metaphors for the Church. Much stress is placed on the call of the entire Church to sanctity—something often over-looked in the immediate post-conciliar period; without a focus on holiness of life, one has no reason to belong to the Church. "One enters into the People of God by faith and Baptism," we read. Furthermore, we find the insight of the Vatican II document *Ad Gentes*: "'All men are called to belong to the new People of God,' so that, in Christ, 'men may form one family and one People of God'" (804). The missionary nature of the Church is thus emphasized, in response to those (even missionaries, oddly enough) who have argued that there is no need to make con-verts.

Church and Eucharist as Body of Christ

The relationship between the ecclesial Body of Christ and the Eucharistic Body of Christ is developed in great depth. Be-ing incorporated into the Body of Christ (the Church) in and though Baptism orients a believer to his Eucharistic Body; fur-ther, receiving the Eucharist makes one ever more fully and perfectly a member of that Body which is the Church (cf. 805). Reading on, we learn that "in the unity of this Body (the Church), there is a diversity of members and functions," but in so marvelous a manner that unity and diversity are strength-ened, not compromised (806). The uniqueness of every call within the Church is thus underscored; and so, there is no need for unhealthy competition among the various roles and ministries within the one Church, all of which exist to build up the one Body. Everything is then put into proper perspec-tive. "The Church is the Body of which Christ is the Head: she lives from him, in him, and for him; he lives with her and in her" (807). How is the Church the Bride of Christ? Christ "loved her and handed himself over for her. He has purified her by his blood and made her the fruitful mother of all God's children" (808). If every Christian, by virtue of Baptism, is a temple of the Holy Spirit, so is the Church, but even more wondrously, for "the Spirit is the soul, as it were, of the Mystical Body, the source of its life" (809). In sum, "the universal Church is seen to be 'a people brought into unity from the unity of the Father, the Son, and the Holy Spirit'" (810).

The Four Marks of the Church

We are next led through a reflection on the four marks, or notes, of the Church. The Church is *one* because "she acknowledges one Lord, confesses one faith, is born of one Baptism, forms only one Body, is given life by the one Spirit," thus causing her to "[surmount] all divisions" (866). The catechism exerts particular care to explain the meaning of *Lumen Gentium's* "subsists in," that is, that it refers to the one Church of Christ and the Catholic Church (870). In answer to troublesome and mischievous theologians, the text teaches clearly that one is to see the realization of the one Church within the boundaries of the Catholic Church. It goes on to discuss the fractured unity of the Church in a way that is both honest and hopeful, relying on the realism of the Council and not the euphoria of the era following.

The Church is *holy* because she has God for her Author, Christ for her Spouse and the Holy Spirit for her source of life. Although the Church is all-holy, she holds within herself sinners, all the while producing saints, of which the Blessed Virgin stands out as the first (cf. 867). The Church is *catholic* because "she proclaims the fullness of the faith. She bears in herself and administers the totality of the means of salvation. She is sent out to all peoples. She speaks to all men. She encompasses all times. She is 'missionary of her very nature'"

(868). That's quite a mouthful, but all that is encompassed in any true understanding of catholicity, while anything less is but a partial truth. Also discussed is the fact that "each particular church [diocese] is 'catholic'" (832) because of its bishop standing in apostolic succession and in communion with the Bishop of Rome and every other Catholic bishop in the world. The text asks the question, "Who belong to the Catholic Church?" It answers by citing *Lumen Gentium* no.14 that speaks of those who "fully . . . accept all the means of salvation given to the Church together with her entire organization" (837). It then continues by dealing with those who have "a certain, although imperfect, communion with the Catholic Church," at which point specific reference is made to the Eastern Orthodox (cf. 838). Clearly taking a cue from Pope John Paul II's *Redemptoris Missio*, the catechism spends much time talking about the importance of missionary activity (849-56).

In presenting the *apostolic* character of the Church, the catechism writes of her foundation on the Twelve Apostles, going on to observe that she is thus "indestructible" and "upheld infallibly in the truth," due to her governance "through Peter and the other apostles, who are present in their successors, the Pope and the college of bishops" (869).

Who Are Christ's Faithful?

The fourth section is concerned with Christ's faithful, which term includes all members of the laity, hierarchy and consecrated life. This diversity of roles is the clearest example of the presence and working of the Holy Spirit within the Church. An excellent explanation is given of "the hierarchical constitution of the Church," taking in the very basic notion of ecclesial ministry in general, with the salutary reminder that "no one can give himself the mandate and the mission to proclaim the

Gospel. The one sent by the Lord does not speak and act on his own authority, but by virtue of Christ's authority; not as a member of the community, but speaking to it in the name of Christ" (874-75). Careful delineation is given to the college of bishops and its relationship to the Church as a whole and to the Pope. The teaching task within the Church is elucidated in regard to the Pope, an ecumenical council and individual bishops, but not for bishops' conferences—contrary to what some theologians have been proposing (888-92).

The ministry of sanctification is located within the ordained ministry (893). Ecclesiastical governance is likewise entrusted to the bishops, who should emulate the example of the Good Shepherd (894-96). Relying on Vatican II and subsequent teaching, the catechism holds that the mission of the laity is primarily toward the world and normally not to be exercised within the Church, except in situations of genuine need (897-903). The task of evangelization (outside the Church) and re-evangelization (within the Church) is something especially geared to the gifts of the laity (904-06). Those in the state of consecrated life, vowed more intimately to divine service and dedicated "to the good of the whole Church" make "public profession of the evangelical counsels of poverty, chastity, and obedience, in a stable state of life recognized by the Church" (944-45). This, of course, is nothing more or less than what we have always believed as Catholics, although not necessarily what some religious would have us think is the current mentality of the Church in regard to their special vocation.

The Communion of Saints

In the discussion on the communion of saints, we are reminded that, called to be saints through Baptism, we are directed toward holy things. As the Eastern liturgy puts it, *Hagia hagiois* (Holy things for the holy). This communion includes fellowship in the faith, sacraments, charisms, common life and charity (949-53). Furthermore, our present communion on earth is inextricably linked to communion with the Church in her three-fold existence: on earth, in purgatory, in heaven. The intercession of the saints and the poor souls benefits us; our request for their intercession acknowledges our bond to them; our prayer for the souls in purgatory and their attention to our needs reveal the bonds which death itself cannot break (954-59).

Finally, our gaze is directed to the Blessed Virgin Mary, Mother and first member of her Son's Church, as she "already shares in the glory of her Son's Resurrection, anticipating the resurrection of all members of his Body," for we believe that she "continues in heaven to exercise her maternal role on behalf of the members of Christ" (974-75). Thus, the Church which has its origins in the eternal plan of God is likewise pointed in the direction of her final goal.

The Forgiveness of Sins

"The Apostles' Creed associates faith in the forgiveness of sins not only with faith in the Holy Spirit, but also . . . in the communion of saints," states the catechism (976). These three realities are found together in the appearance of the Risen Christ on Easter night as he conferred the gift of the Holy Spirit on his chosen band of apostles (the infant Church), precisely to bring about and to guarantee until the end of time the forgiveness of sins.

Such forgiveness is encountered the first time in the Sacrament of Baptism, whereby the sin of Adam is eradicated as well as any subsequent actual or personal sins (if the person being baptized is an adult). Sins committed after Baptism are remitted through the Sacrament of Penance which many of the Fathers of the Church dubbed a second Baptism since it does for the already-baptized what Baptism does for the not-yet-baptized. Due to the *power of the keys* conferred on the Church by Jesus Christ, "there is no offense, however serious, that the Church cannot forgive," declares the catechism. "There is no one, however wicked and guilty, who may not confidently hope for forgiveness, provided his repentance is honest," it asserts consolingly (982). Quoting St. John Chrysostom, the text reminds us that "priests have received from God a power that he has given neither to angels nor to archangels . . . God above confirms what priests do here below" (983).

Resurrection and Everlasting Life

Having been incorporated into Christ's death and resurrection through Baptism and having benefitted from his saving grace in Penance throughout one's life, the believer (in the words of the Creed) professes one's faith in "resurrection of the dead on the last day and in life everlasting" (988). This final resurrection, however, is not merely spiritual; rather, "even our 'mortal body' (Rom 8:11) will come to life again" (990). This is critical to appreciate nowadays for, citing Tertullian, the catechism teaches that "the flesh is the hinge of salvation." Furthermore, "we believe in God who is creator of the flesh; we believe in the Word made flesh in order to redeem the flesh; we believe in the resurrection of the flesh, the fufillment of both the creation and the redemption of the flesh" (1015). By means of a brief historical survey, the catechism reviews how God gradually revealed this truth to the People of God, reaching a highwater mark in Second Maccabees and in the teachings of the Pharisees, with whom Our Lord was in doctrinal agreement on this central tenet. All this was by way of preface to Christ's own Resurrection; indeed, "to be a witness to Christ is to be a 'witness to his Resurrection'" (Acts 1:22), for "we shall rise like Christ, with him, and through him" (995).

This all leads to the logical question, "How do the dead rise?" First of all, what does it mean to "rise"? The catechism explains that "in death, the separation of the soul from the body, the human body decays and the soul goes to meet God, while awaiting its reunion with its glorified body. God, in his almighty power, will definitively grant incorruptible life to our bodies by reuniting them with our souls, through the power of Jesus' Resurrection" (997). All men will rise, we are told, while the "how" of it all "exceeds our imagination" and is open "only to faith." The text goes on to note that "our participation in the Eucharist already gives us a foretaste of Christ's transfiguration of our bodies" (1000), as preparation for the last day— Christ's Parousia or final coming in glory (1001). The emphasis on the real, bodily, corporeal nature of the risen body is important since some thinkers today have reduced the risen life to no more than a vague kind of shadowy existence; the ultimate and normal mode of existence for those possessed of a human nature is life in a body, to which the presence of Our Lord and His Blessed Mother in their glorified bodies in heaven now attests.

While observing that "in a sense bodily death is natural," the catechism also stresses that from the perspective of faith, death is seen as "the wages of sin," as St. Paul put it to the Romans (1006). "Death is transformed by Christ," we read, most especially because of his enduring it "in an act of complete and free submission to his Father's will." Therefore, "the obedience of Jesus has transformed the curse of death into a blessing" (1009). This is seen most clearly in the Christian attitude toward death, crystallized in the funeral liturgy: "For your faithful people, Lord, life is changed, not ended." The phase of pilgrimage thus ends and is taken up into man's final goal—eternal life. The catechism takes special aim at theological or philosophical theories that would fail to take account of the finality and irrepeatability of human life and death. Very bluntly, it says, "There is no 'reincarnation' after death" (1012-13).

This reflection ends with an encouragement to avail oneself of all the aids of traditional spirituality in preparing for one's death. Thus we are reminded of the petition of the Litany of the Saints that the Lord would deliver us "from a sudden and unforeseen death," as well our daily prayer to the Virgin to "intercede for us 'at the hour of our death.'" It also urges us to have recourse to the intercession of St. Joseph, "the patron of a happy death" (1014).

Having met death, what has one to look forward to? Life eternal. But in what does that consist? Immediately upon death, each person experiences a "particular judgment" that seals his destiny for eternity. "Those who die in God's grace and friendship and are perfectly purified live forever with Christ" (1022-23). This living forever occurs in the place we call heaven, which "is the ultimate end and fulfillment of the deepest human longings, the state of supreme, definitive happiness" (1024). "To live in heaven is 'to be with Christ'" (1025). "This mystery of blessed communion with God and all who are in Christ is beyond all understanding and description" (1027); this experience of heavenly glory we call "the beatific vision" (1028).

Next we consider "all who die in God's grace and friendship, but still imperfectly purified, are indeed assured of their eternal salvation." These souls "undergo purification, so as to achieve the holiness necessary to enter the joy of heaven" (1030); "this final purification of the elect" is traditionally called purgatory and is "entirely different from the punishment of the damned" (1031). On behalf of the poor souls, we are advised to pray, especially through the offering of the Eucharistic Sacrifice. "The Church also commends almsgiving, indulgences, and works of penance undertaken on behalf of the dead" (1032)—in response to those who have argued for twenty-five years that such efforts are either useless or not in keeping with *contemporary* Catholic approaches.

Even less modern, so to speak, is the insistence on the reality of eternal punishment. "This state of definitive self-exclusion from communion with God and the blessed is called 'hell'" (1033). "The teaching of the Church affirms the existence of hell and its eternity. Immediately after death the souls of those who die in a state of mortal sin descend into hell . . . The chief punishment of hell is eternal separation from God" (1035).

Why does the Church adhere to such a teaching? First of all, because it is part of divine Revelation, but also to serve as "a call to the responsibility" (for man to use his freedom wisely "in view of his eternal destiny") and "a call to conversion" (following the lead of the Lord who urged men to "enter by the narrow gate," not the wide one that "leads to destruction") (1036). Finally, we read that "God predestines no one to go to hell; for this, a willful turning away from God (a mortal sin) is necessary, and persistence in it until the end" (1037). This position of the Church, then, is presented in a truly positive and holistic fashion, as is appropriate.

Following the general resurrection comes the final judgment. "The holy Roman Church firmly believes and confesses that on the Day of Judgment all men will appear in their own bodies before Christ's tribunal to render an account of their own deeds" (1059). With the result that "the Kingdom of God will come in its fullness. Then the just will reign with Christ forever, glorified in body and soul, and the material universe itself will be transformed. God will then be 'all in all' (1 Cor 15:28), in eternal life" (1060). This focus is especially valuable in a time when catechesis and preaching alike have failed to give adequate attention to a life for man beyond our present existence.

Amen

Knowing what God has in store for those who love him and believe in what his Church proposes in the Creed, the People of God end their profession of faith with an enthusiastic "Amen," which thus "confirms its first words: 'I believe'" (1064).

DISCUSSION QUESTIONS

Part One: The Profession of Faith
1. Should a creed be recited in the singular ("I believe") or the plural ("We believe")?

2. How do we come to know God?

3. How has God revealed Himself to man?

4. Explain the two facets of Apostolic Tradition and their interrelatedness.

5. How are we to view the Old and New Testaments?

6. What is faith?

7. What are the implications of having faith in One God?

8. Explain the meaning of the Trinity.

9. Why did God create us?

10. How are we to regard angels?

11. How and why did God create man and woman?

12. Jesus (the Savior) is called "Christ," "Son of God" and "Lord." What do these titles signify?

13. State the four reasons for the Incarnation.

A TOUR OF THE CATHOLIC CATECHISM

14. Explain the two natures of Jesus.

15. What is the Virgin Mary's place in the plan of salvation?

16. Why is it important to learn about the mysteries of Christ's life?

17. How does Christ's death fit into God's plan of salvation?

18. Why did Christ institute the Eucharist?

19. What did the Resurrection of Jesus accomplish?

20. What does Christ's ascension mean for us?

21. Why must the Church be alert until Christ comes again in glory?

22. In what areas of the Church are we to recognize the Holy Spirit?

23. List the signs and symbols of the Holy Spirit.

24. Explain how the Holy Spirit: a) prepares God's people for the coming of the Savior, b) realizes God's plan of salvation through Mary, and c) fulfills God's plan through Jesus.

25. How is the mission of Christ and the Holy Spirit brought to completion in the Church?

26. What is the Church's mission?

27. How are the members of the universal Church linked to one another?

28. State and define the four marks of the Church.

29. Who belongs to the Catholic Church? What are their roles in the Church?

30. What is meant by "the communion of saints"?

31. What is Mary's role in the Church?

32. How are our sins forgiven?

33. Why does the catechism teach that the flesh is the "hinge of salvation"?

34. What is meant by the "resurrection of the body"?

35. What does "particular judgment" mean at the hour of one's death?

36. What is meant by hell? Why would someone deserve this eternal punishment?

37. Explain the difference between "particular judgment" and "final judgment."

38. Why do we end the Creed with "Amen"?

part two:
THE CELEBRATION OF THE CHRISTIAN MYSTERY

In the earthly liturgy we share in a foretaste of that heavenly liturgy which is celebrated in the Holy City of Jerusalem . . .
Constitution on the Sacred Liturgy

part two:
THE CELEBRATION OF THE CHRISTIAN MYSTERY

SECTION ONE: THE SACRAMENTAL ECONOMY

I n the days of the Church, Christ "acts through the sacraments." This "'sacramental economy'" has God the Father as its "source and goal" (1076-77). In other words, he is the One "source of all the blessings," as well as the ultimate goal of our prayer and our entire existence, a process begun and guided by Almighty God in having conferred on us "filial adoption" (1110).

Liturgy: Work of the Trinity

The catechism describes the work of Christ in the liturgy, noting that the point of departure is the glorified Christ, who "by giving the Holy Spirit to the apostles, entrusted to them his power of sanctifying," which power is passed on to their successors as well. "This 'apostolic succession' structures the whole liturgical life of the Church and is itself sacramental, [which sacramentality is] handed on by the sacrament of Holy Orders" (1087). Hence, we are made to recall that the hierarchical structure of the Church is not a mere appendage or necessary evil; rather, it lies at the very essence of ecclesiality. The Risen Christ communicates his life to the Church on earth through the Church's liturgy, by which "the pilgrim Church already participates, as by a foretaste, in the heavenly liturgy" (1111).

An indispensable role in the liturgy is played by the Holy Spirit: "He prepares the Church to encounter her Lord; he recalls and makes Christ manifest to the faith of the assembly. By his transforming power, he makes the mystery of Christ present here and now. Finally the Spirit of communion unites the Church to the life and mission of Christ" (1092). A strong stress is placed on the "today" of liturgical action (1095); that is, what we do in the sacraments is not a mere act of remembering. Rather, it consists in the traditional Jewish notion of *memorial*, whereby the present act of recalling truly brings about a present reality. As the catechism has it, "The Holy Spirit is the Church's living memory" (1099). It is also worth noting here the excellent discussion on the connections between Jewish and Christian liturgy (1096).

The Paschal Mystery and the Sacraments

The text then moves into a consideration of "the paschal mystery in the Church's sacraments," observing that "the whole liturgical life of the Church revolves around the Eucharistic sacrifice and the sacraments" (1113). The seven sacraments are listed and their origin in Christ is affirmed; that divine institution, however, is carefully explained, lest someone walk away with an unhistorical or crude notion of the process. The Church, "by the power of the Spirit who guides her 'into all truth' (Jn 16:13), has gradually recognized this treasure received from Christ and, as the faithful steward of God's mysteries, has determined its 'dispensation'" (1117). These visible signs of invisible grace "bear fruit in those who receive them with the required dispositions" (1131); these actions express the priestly nature of the entire Church, but "the ordained minister is the sacramental bond that ties the liturgical action to what the apostles said and did and, through them, to the words and actions of Christ, the source and foundation of the sacraments" (1120). Restating traditional doctrine, the catechism teaches that three sacraments (Baptism, Confirmation and Holy Orders) "confer, in addition to grace, a sacramental *character* or 'seal,'" which is "indelible," so that these sacraments can never be erased or repeated (1121).

Faith and salvation are integral to the sacraments. "The sacraments strengthen faith and express it" (1133); this faith exists in the Church before it does in an individual believer (1124). "The fruit of sacramental life is both personal and ecclesial." The first aspect makes one live wholly "for God in Christ Jesus"; the second brings about for the Church "an increase in charity and in her mission of witness" (1134). Also restated is the Church's perennial teaching on the way sacraments "work"— "by virtue of the saving work of Christ, accomplished once for all" (*ex opere operato*) and hence are not effected by the action of man, but "by the power of God." Quickly, the text affirms that sacramental validity does not depend on the "personal holiness of the minister." At the same time, we are reminded that "the fruits of the sacraments also depend on the disposition of the one who receives them" (1128).

Celebrating the Liturgy

The following section takes up details of a more practical order, but one grounded in theological truths.

1. *Who celebrates the liturgy?* The answer: *Totus Christus,*

the whole Christ, which refers to the fact that in each and every liturgical action, the entire Church is present, including (and even especially) those who are currently participating in the liturgy of heaven (1136). This understanding is critical to recapture if we are to get ourselves back on track liturgically, returning to a true sense of the sacred.

2. *How is the liturgy celebrated?* Taking a sociological fact of life as a starting point, the catechism makes a profoundly religious application. "As a social being, man needs signs and symbols to communicate with others, through language, gestures, and actions. The same holds true for his relationship with God" (1146). Beyond that, Christianity (as an incarnational religion) takes seriously the human and the physical. "Integrated into the world of faith and taken up by the power of the Holy Spirit, these cosmic elements, human rituals, and gestures of remembrance of God become bearers of the saving and sanctifying action of Christ" (1189).

The place of God's Word in the liturgy is emphasized, as is the importance of good sacred music that elevates the human spirit (1153-58). An extensive section deals with holy images, obviously in response to neo-iconoclasts. "Sacred images in our churches and homes are intended to awaken and nourish our faith in the mystery of Christ." Offering a clear catechesis on what is involved here, it says, "Through the icon of Christ and his works of salvation, it is he whom we adore. Through sacred images of the holy Mother of God, of the angels and of the saints, we venerate the person represented" (1192). Having such images visible in the midst of the liturgical assembly is seen as a way of reminding us of the presence of that great "cloud of witnesses" described in the Epistle to the Hebrews and of their participation in the present liturgical action (1161). So much for those who wish to banish such elements from our church buildings.

3. *When is the liturgy celebrated?* Once more, an emphasis is placed on the *today* of all such events. A marvelous treatment is given of "Sunday, the 'Lord's Day,' [which] is the principal day for the celebration of the Eucharist because it is the day of the Resurrection. It is the pre-eminent day of the liturgical assembly, the day of the Christian family, and the day of joy and rest from work" (1193). Each item demands careful analysis and reflection, especially in the United States where so many of these elements have been forgotten or ignored.

Flowing from the centrality of the Lord's Day and the liturgical reenactment of the paschal mystery is the Church's liturgical year, which "unfolds the whole mystery of Christ" (1194). Keeping the memory of the Blessed Virgin, first of all, and also of the other saints is critically important since in this way "the Church on earth shows that she is united with the liturgy of heaven. She gives glory to Christ for having accomplished his salvation in his glorified members; their example encourages her on her way to the Father" (1195). This is another direct response to some who have argued, even passionately, against maintaining the cult of the saints.

A superb exposition is given on the Liturgy of the Hours, along with an encouragement to return this prayer to all members of the Church, not just clergy or religious. Also mentioned is that the Hours should be seen as "an extension of the Eucharistic celebration" and, furthermore, that this prayer-form does not exclude "various devotions of the People of God, especially adoration and worship of the Blessed Sacrament," but actually calls for their incorporation into the liturgy "in a complementary way" (1178).

4. *Where should liturgy be celebrated?* While recalling Our Lord's teaching that Christian worship occurs in spirit and in

truth and hence, that it is not bound to an exclusive place, the catechism realistically continues thus: "In its earthly state the Church needs places where the community can gather together. Our visible churches, holy places, are images of the holy city, the heavenly Jerusalem, toward which we are making our way on pilgrimage" (1198). These houses of God on earth should, by their beauty and sense of holiness, remind us of heaven— all of these points, necessary reaffirmations of the importance of sacred places in the life of the Church.

The section concludes with a fine presentation on "liturgical diversity and the unity of the mystery." The various rites of the Church, reflecting her diversity of cultures, are mutually enriching (1200). In discussing "cultural adaptation," the catechism very honestly says that "cultural adaptation also requires a conversion of heart and even, where necessary, a breaking with ancestral customs incompatible with the Catholic faith" (1206). Therefore, discernment is needed, for not everything can be brought into Christian worship in an uncritical manner, lest the Faith itself be compromised or eviscerated. "The criterion that assures unity amid the diversity of liturgical traditions is fidelity to the apostolic Tradition, i.e., the communion in the faith and the sacraments received from the apostles, a communion that is both signified and guaranteed by apostolic succession" (1209).

SECTION TWO:
THE SEVEN SACRAMENTS OF THE CHURCH

The second major division of the worship section of the *Catechism of the Catholic Church* is concerned with the seven sacraments, which "give birth and increase (Baptism, Confirmation, Eucharist), healing (Penance and Sacrament of Sick) and mission (Matrimony and Holy Orders) to the Christian's life of faith. There is thus a certain resemblance between the stages of natural life and the stages of the spiritual life" (1210). Within the overall sacramental structure, however, there is a hierarchy, so that (as St. Thomas Aquinas teaches) the Eucharist should be seen as "the Sacrament of sacraments" since "all the other sacraments are ordered to it as to their end" (1211).

BAPTISM

With the general context in place, we can now see where Baptism fits, namely within that grouping of sacraments dealing with birth and growth or commonly referred to as the sacraments of initiation, which "lay the *foundation*" of every Christian life" (1212); and within that schema, Baptism holds a pre-eminent place since it is truly "the gateway to life in the Spirit *(vitae spiritualis ianua),* and the door which gives access to the other sacraments." Furthermore, through it "we are freed from sin and reborn as sons of God; we become members of Christ, are incorporated into the Church and made sharers in her mission" (1213). That's quite a mouthful and calls for a good amount of dissection.

The various names for this sacrament are treated (Baptism, bath of regeneration and renewal in the Holy Spirit, illumination), for each offers a particular angle from which to study this multi-faceted mystery. The primary symbol for Baptism, of course, is water. The catechism discusses its natural meaning which conveys the notion of life (when it comes from a living spring) and death (when of stupendous proportions, as in a sea); both are to be perceived in this sacrament that brings death to sin and life to God. Various foreshadowings of Baptism are likewise presented, especially the passage of the Chosen People through the Red Sea (1217-22). "All the Old Covenant prefigurations find their fulfillment in Christ Jesus," with his baptism by John in the Jordan; that, in turn, becomes paradigmatic for Christians as the disciples are commissioned by the Risen Christ to evangelize and baptize all nations in the name of the Triune God (1223).

Christian Initiation

A brief history of the sacrament is given and followed by a detailed explanation of the process of Christian initiation: "proclamation of the Word, acceptance of the Gospel entailing conversion, profession of faith, Baptism itself, the outpouring of the Holy Spirit, and admission to Eucharistic communion" (1229). The catechism notes that these are the necessary elements, regardless of whether we are talking about a unified catechumenate that precedes the sacraments or a post-baptismal catechumenate, as when infant baptism is the case. Without taking an overt position, the catechism does consistently come down on the side of the contemporary discussion that favors restoring the order of sacraments to that of Baptism, Confirmation, Eucharist; it does so simply by repeatedly offering that as the appropriate sequence without, however, proscribing what has developed (1233).

Since the Church has always subscribed to the principle of *lex orandi, lex credendi*—"the law of prayer is the law of belief"—not surprisingly does the text go on to analyze the constituent parts of the baptismal rite (1234-45), in order to plumb the depths of the truths to be apprehended. The sign of the cross, the proclamation of the Word of God (wherein great play is given to the role of faith which is stirred up and responds), exorcism (since Baptism signifies liberation from sin and its instigator, the Devil), confessing the Faith of the Church, consecration of baptismal water, the baptism proper (a preference seems to be indicated for triple immersion), anointing with chrism, clothing with the white garment, presentation of the lighted candle, recitation of the Our Father (since the neophyte is now truly a child of God). The catechism also observes that in the Eastern Churches sacramental communion is then administered (even to infants), to highlight the linkage between Baptism and Eucharist; it notes that this connection is even maintained in the West by bringing the child to the altar during the praying of the Our Father. All concludes with the solemn blessing; the text says that during the Baptism of newborns, the blessing of the mother holds a special place, not quite the situation in the English ritual that has the mother's blessing as but one of the three invocations for the solemn blessing (1245).

Requirements for Baptism

Who can be baptized? "Every person not yet baptized and only such a person is able to be baptized" (1246). In other words, baptism cannot be repeated, and only humans (not Cabbage Patch dolls or cats!) are eligible recipients. In discussing catechumens, the catechism stresses that these people "are already joined to the Church" (1249). The treatment on infant baptism is careful to handle several important points: (1) Infants are "born with a fallen human nature and tainted by original sin"; (2) "The sheer gratuitousness of the grace of salvation is particularly manifest in infant Baptism"; (3) Since Baptism confers on an infant "the priceless grace of becoming a child of God," the sacrament should be received within a time "shortly after birth" (1250). All these items were in the Catholic consciousness (even among non-practicing Catholics) only two decades ago, but conviction about them has often been eroded, even among the devout, because of defective and at times malevolent catechesis—hence their clear restatement here.

An excellent presentation is made on the relationship between faith and baptism (1253-55) for candidates, parents, godparents and the whole Church. The ordinary ministers of Baptism are given as bishops and priests (and deacons as well for the Latin Rite); extraordinary ministers include anyone (baptized or not) who, in an emergency, intends to do what the Church intends and uses water and the proper Trinitarian formula (1256). By the way, clear mention is made that a valid formula requires the use of the words "the Father, the Son, and the Holy Spirit" (1278); thus, efforts to circumvent "sexist" language by resorting to alternatives like "Creator, Redeemer, Sanctifier" would result in invalid baptisms. After all, the Trinity into which we are baptized is a trinity of interrelated persons, not of mere differentiated functions.

The Necessity of Baptism and Its Effects

While holding for the necessity of baptism, the catechism is very nuanced here. Yes, indeed, "God has bound salvation to the sacrament of Baptism, but *he himself* is not bound by his sacraments" (emphasis added, 1257). What is being said and not being said here? Baptism is the normal means of bringing a person into a saving relationship with Jesus Christ, but God can choose to use other means in his inscrutable wisdom and providence. Scholars of St. Thomas Aquinas will quickly pick this up as the teaching of the Angelic Doctor. This position thus allows for the salvation of those who, through no fault of their own, have not heard the Gospel and so cannot respond with faith and the request for baptism (1260). It also comes to grips with the condition of children who die without Baptism by asserting that "the Church can only entrust them to the mercy of God . . . who desires that all men should be saved, and Jesus' tenderness toward children which caused him to say: 'Let the children come to me, do not hinder them'" (1261). Apparently, the catechism wants to put to rest the theological speculation that gave rise to the theory of limbo, a theory which many treated with the respect and authority due to dogma.

The catechism teaches that there are two principal effects of Baptism: remission of sins (negative) and new birth and life in the Holy Spirit (positive). Once the first is effected, room now exists for God's life, "sanctifying grace, the grace of *justification* that imparts the theological virtues of faith, hope and charity; grants the gifts of the Holy Spirit; and provides for growth in goodness through the moral virtues—all of this happening as a result of the reception of Baptism (1265-66). In all honesty, one must ask when was the last time a catechesis or homily on Baptism was heard to present all these truths, instead of the more sociological "incorpora[tion] into the Church" approach.

Once sin has been removed and divine life has been given, one is "incorporated into the Church" (1267), but things must be viewed in priority order. Now, part of the Church, the baptized "is called to be subject to others, to serve them in the communion of the Church, and to 'obey and submit' to the Church leaders, holding them in respect and affection." Such responsibilities also bring in their wake certain rights, namely, "to receive the sacraments, to be nourished with the Word of God and to be sustained by the other spiritual helps of the Church" (1269). Flowing from one's baptism is likewise the duty and privilege "[to] participate in the apostolic and missionary activity of the People of God" (1270). We are also reminded that "Baptism constitutes the foundation of communion among all Christians, including those who are not yet in full communion with the Catholic Church"; therefore, Baptism is, in truth, "the sacramental bond of unity" (1271).

The section ends with reference made to the "seal of the Lord" of Baptism which is nothing other than the *seal* or *character* of the Lord imprinted on the soul of the baptized, destining one for eternal life. As the Roman Canon puts it, such have been "marked with the sign of faith," and in that faith is awaited "the blessed vision of God—the consummation of faith—and . . . the hope of resurrection" (1274).

Judaism and Typological Language

Perhaps a digression here is in order as we read words like "type," "foreshadowing" and "prefigurement." Not infrequently, Jews express dismay over such concepts because, in their opinion, this approach relegates Judaism to the status of a mere preparatory phase in salvation history at best, or one that is totally useless at worst. Understood properly, that should not be the case. There is no doubt that Christian doctrine understands Jesus to be the definitive Word of the Father to the human race (cf. Heb 1:1-2). Indeed, the Fathers of the Church taught that every passage of the Hebrew Scriptures did, in fact, point toward him and find its fulfillment in him. However, this only makes sense since we believe that he is precisely the One for whom the people of the promise were waiting and being prepared. That much Jews today should be brought to understand. On the other hand, this in no way devalues the present condition of Judaism which, St. Paul holds (Rom 9-11), retains its validity as a means of salvation for the Jews until the end of time—even while Christianity is the means of salvation for the Gentiles.

CONFIRMATION

"Baptism, the Eucharist, and the sacrament of Confirmation together constitute the 'sacraments of Christian initiation,' whose unity must be safeguarded." Thus begins the treatment of Confirmation with a caution repeated many times during the entire section—a nervousness about the practice of the Latin Rite that may suggest a change in discipline is in the offing. Immediately following this is the strong statement that "it must be explained to the faithful that the reception of the sacrament of Confirmation is necessary for the completion of baptismal grace." Why? Because "by the sacrament of Confirmation, [the baptized] are more perfectly bound to the Church and are enriched with a special strength of the Holy Spirit. Hence they are, as true witnesses of Christ, more strictly obliged to spread and defend the faith by word and deed" (1285).

Situating Confirmation

Confirmation is placed in the total picture of "the economy of salvation," in both Covenants. Citing Old Testament texts, the catechism notes that the coming of the Spirit, however, would reach its fullness in and through the Messiah and, through him, "be communicated to *the whole messianic people*" (1286-87), which event occurred on the Day of Pentecost. Tracing out the history of the Sacrament in the Church, it is said that "very early, the better to signify the gift of the Holy Spirit, an anointing with perfumed oil (*chrism*) was added to the laying on of hands," from which chrism comes the name of "Christian," that is, "anointed" (like Christ himself). The Sacrament has different names in the Churches of East and West, highlighting different but complementary notions. In the East, it is called *"Chrismation,"* precisely to stress the act of making one into another Christ through the holy anointing; "in the West, *Confirmation* suggests both the ratification of Baptism . . . and the strengthening of baptismal grace—both fruits of the Holy Spirit" (1289).

The catechism offers a splendid analysis of the two different traditions between East and West in regard to this sacrament (*East*: Baptism, Confirmation and Eucharist received, even by infants, all within a unified rite performed by a priest; *West*: the temporal separation of the sacraments for infants and, in some cases, even the inversion of Confirmation [usually reserved to a bishop] and Eucharist). Citing St. Cyprian, it mentions how he saw the unity of Baptism and Confirmation, all the while seeing the distinctiveness between them, so that he spoke of them as a "double sacrament" (1290). The text summarizes the pluses of both practices: "The practice of the Eastern Churches gives greater emphasis to the unity of Christian initiation. That of the Latin Church more clearly expresses the communion of the new Christian with the bishop as guarantor and servant of the unity, catholicity and apostolicity of his Church, and hence the connection with the apostolic origins of Christ's Church" (1292).

The Liturgy of Confirmation

The signs and symbols of Confirmation are reflected upon, with special emphasis on the "mark" or s*eal* conferred. "A seal," we read, "is a symbol of a person, a sign of personal authority, or ownership of an object. Hence soldiers were marked with their leader's seal and slaves with their master's." Therefore, we truly belong to Christ, which fact also provides "the promise of divine protection in the great eschatological trial" (1295-96). Going through the rite, the catechism observes that to demonstrate the relation of Confirmation to Baptism, when the two sacraments are celebrated separately, "the Liturgy of Confirmation begins with the renewal of baptismal promises and the profession of faith by the confirmands" (1298). The unity of the sacraments is also brought out by having Confirmation celebrated within the context of the Eucharistic Sacrifice (1321).

The imposition of hands, of course, an ancient and apostolic gesture, "has signified the gift of the Spirit" (1299). "The essential rite of Confirmation is anointing the forehead of the baptized with sacred chrism (in the East other sense organs as well), together with laying on of the minister's hand and the words: '*Accipe signaculum doni Spiritus Sancti*' (Be sealed with the Gift of the Holy Spirit) in the Roman Rite, or 'The seal of the gift that is the Holy Spirit' in the Byzantine rite" (1320). "The sign of peace that concludes the rite of the sacrament signifies and demonstrates ecclesial communion with the bishop and with all the faithful" (1301).

The Why and Who of Confirmation

Why is Confirmation so important? Consider the effects: "It roots us more deeply in the divine filiation which makes us cry, 'Abba! Father!' (Rom 8:15); it unites us more firmly to Christ; it increases the gifts of the Holy Spirit in us; it renders our bond with the Church more perfect; it gives us a special strength of the Holy Spirit" to do the work of Christ and His Church, to "confess the name of Christ boldly, and never to be ashamed of the Cross" (1303). Again, one must regrettably ask when such a list of effects formed part of our sacramental catechesis in the past two decades in the United States.

Who can receive this sacrament? "A candidate for Confirmation who has attained the age of reason must profess the faith, be in the state of grace, have the intention of receiving the sacrament, and be prepared to assume the role of disciple and witness to Christ, both within the ecclesial community and in temporal affairs" (1319). Several times the catechism talks about "the age of discretion" being the normal age for the reception of Confirmation (1307). What about making a personal decision for Christ, about which we have heard so much in this country and so the delay to the teenage years? Taking direct aim at such theories, the catechism warns: "Although Confirmation is sometimes called the 'sacrament of Christian maturity,' we must not confuse adult faith with the adult age of natural growth, nor forget that the baptismal grace is a grace of free, unmerited election and *does not need 'ratification' to become effective*" (emphasis added, 1308).

In what should catechesis for Confirmation consist? It should "[lead] the Christian toward a more intimate union with Christ and a more lively familiarity with the Holy Spirit—his actions, his gifts, and his biddings—in order to be more capable of assuming the apostolic responsibilities of Christian life. To this end catechesis for Confirmation should strive to awaken a sense of belonging to the Church of Jesus Christ, *the universal Church as well as the parish community*. The latter bears special responsibility for the preparation of *confirmands*" (emphasis added, 1309). Again, we see the gaps in American theory and practice.

The text notes that a sponsor is needed as a spiritual guide and that, ideally, it should be the same person as for Baptism to mark better the unity of the two sacraments (1311). "The ordinary minister of Confirmation is the bishop," we are reminded. Then follows a restatement of the divergent approaches of East and West. Latin-rite bishops are presented with an admonition that they take seriously their obligation to administer this sacrament personally and not delegate this power frivolously, "mindful that the celebration of Confirmation has been temporally separated from Baptism" (1313).

With Confirmation as "the gift of Christ's fullness" (1314) well handled, it might be good to call attention to the effort of this catechism truly to be the catechism of the *whole* Church, both East and West. Repeatedly, we are given the theological perspectives of the Churches of East and West and led to appreciate our catholicity, whereby both traditions are complementary and mutually enriching. Not by accident has this text been promulgated by the Pope who has urged the entire Church once more to *breathe with both lungs.*

EUCHARIST

In incredibly complete fashion, the catechism treats of the Eucharist, "source and summit of the Church's life" in twenty pages! The various names are given for this "sacrament of sacraments" (Eucharist, Lord's Supper, Breaking of the Bread, Eucharistic Assembly, Holy and Divine Liturgy, Communion, Holy Mass), along with the significance of each as each fills out some element of the total mystery, which would be difficult if not impossible to capture with only one title (1328-32).

Eucharist in Salvation History

A thorough presentation is made on the signs of bread and wine, including their place in worship throughout salvation history—in both covenants. It is noted that "the first announcement of the Eucharist divided the disciples, just as the announcement of the passion scandalized them" (1335). This point is made because the text then goes on to a profound analysis of Catholic Eucharistic doctrine, which cannot but be a source of division where faith and grace are not present.

In speaking of Our Blessed Lord's institution of the Eucharist in the context of the Jewish Passover, it is said that "Jesus gave His definitive meaning" to this feast. Lest Jews see this as but another example of Christian "replacement" or "fulfillment" theology, it should not be missed that even the Eucharist is not presented as final. In reality, although the Eucharist "fulfills the Jewish Passover," it "anticipates the final Passover of the Church in the glory of the Kingdom" (1340); in other words, all ritual actions have a dimension to them that is but temporary, destined to be subsumed into the Eternal, in a time and place where signs and symbols will not be needed.

Perhaps responding to implicit attacks on liturgical reform, the following section is entitled, "The Mass of All the Ages," that outlines the basic structure of the sacred liturgy in every age: the Liturgy of the Word (composed of "the writings of the prophets" and "the memoirs of the apostles") (1349) and the Liturgy of the Eucharist, forming together "a single and same act of worship" (1346), just as the Risen Christ envisioned and accomplished it in his Emmaus journey with the disciples (1347).

In analyzing the various liturgical roles, the text stresses the active participation of all the faithful, but stresses the fact that Christ himself is "the principal actor of the Eucharist" (1348) and this presidency of his can be represented "only [by] priests validly ordained" for only they can "consecrate the bread and wine so that they become the Body and Blood of the Lord" (1411). The constituent parts of the Liturgy of the Eucharist are explained in summary but complete manner. As if to answer in a definitive manner some liturgists who argue for various "moments" when the transformation of elements occurs, the catechism teaches unequivocally, "The eucharistic presence of Christ begins *at the moment of the consecration*" (emphasis added). Anticipating another disputed point of recent years, it goes on to say that this presence "continues as long as the eucharistic species remain" (1377).

Eucharist as Sacrifice
The fifth major division of this treatise is concerned with

"the sacramental sacrifice," reflected upon as thanksgiving, memorial, presence. The Eucharist is, first and foremost, the Church's sacrifice of praise offered to the Father "in the name of all creation . . . by Christ, and with Him . . . and in Him" (1361), which is why it is the most perfect form of worship possible. In considering the Eucharist as a memorial sacrifice, the catechism stresses that "this is not only the remembrance of past events"; on the contrary, they "become in a certain manner present and actual." The explanation continues: "It is thus that Israel understands her liberation from Egypt: Each time that Passover is celebrated, the events of the Exodus are rendered present to the memory of believers, so that they might conform their life to those events." Similarly, as *Lumen Gentium* teaches, "every time that the Sacrifice of the Cross by which Christ our Passover was sacrificed is celebrated on the altar, the work of our redemption is accomplished" (1364). Hence, it is precisely because the Eucharist "is the memorial of the Passover of Christ, [that it] is also a sacrifice" (1366). In the entire discussion on the Eucharist as sacrifice, the catechism relies heavily on the Council of Trent (at least five citations in two pages), implicitly and clearly asserting the on-going validity of the Tridentine doctrine of the Mass.

In addition to being the sacrifice of Christ, the Mass is also the sacrifice of the Church, "which is the Body of Christ. . . . The sacrifice of Christ present on the altar gives to all generations of Christians the possibility of being united to His offering" (1368). Beyond that, "the whole Church is united to the offering and to the intercession of Christ," thus presenting the rationale for intercessory prayer within the Eucharistic prayer itself (1369). Referring specifically to the mention of the Pope at this time in the liturgy, the text observes that he "is associated with every celebration of the Eucharist where he is named as the sign and servant of the unity of the Universal Church." Offering the Eucharist in union with the whole Christ (which is the whole Church) also demands turning attention to the saints, who participate now in the liturgy of heaven. In a lovely line, we are reminded that "in the Eucharist, the Church—with Mary—is as if at the foot of the Cross, united to the offering and intercession of Christ" (1370).

Eucharist as Real Presence

Turning to the matter of presence, the catechism takes account of the various modes of Christ's presence in the world and in the Church but goes on to make its own the line from *Sacrosanctum Concilium*, which teaches, "But to the highest degree, He is present under the eucharistic species." In case the teaching is missed, it is repeated that this presence "is unique." Once more, the text repeats a teaching of Trent to explain just why the emphasis on the uniqueness of the Eucharistic mystery, for in it "are contained truly, really and substantially the Body and Blood, together with the soul and divinity of Our Lord Jesus Christ, and, consequently, the whole Christ" (1373-74). This marvelous presence comes about "by the conversion of the bread and wine into the Body and Blood of Christ" as a result of the "efficacy of the Word of Christ and of the action of the Holy Spirit to effect this change" (1375).

How is this phenomenon to be understood and explained? Falling back on Trent again, the text reads, "By the consecration of the bread and wine is effected the change of the whole substance of the bread into the Body of Christ Our Lord and of the whole substance of the wine into His Blood; this change, the Catholic Church has rightly and exactly called *transubstantiation*" (1376). As the Gallup Poll finds 70% of every-Sunday-communicants confused about or rejecting the Catholic doctrine of the Eucharist, how necessary is this restatement. If this is truly the Body of Christ, then follow the necessity of worship and the external signs of reverence; particular mention is made of genuflection for the Western Church and the profound bow for the East, as well as other signs of devotion and adoration (1378). Quoting Pope Paul VI's *Mysterium Fidei*, the text singles out one devotion for special notice: "The visit to the Blessed Sacrament is a proof of gratitude, a sign of love and a duty of adoration toward Christ our Lord" (1418).

As we are led to reflect on the Eucharist as the paschal Banquet, it is recalled for us that the altar is a kind of dual symbol, "the altar of sacrifice and the table of the Lord," in both instances representing Christ himself who is "at one and the same time present as the Victim offered for our reconciliation and the heavenly food which is given to us" (1382). Because of the greatness of this mystery, proper preparation is required, including the Eucharistic fast (1387), but especially freedom from serious sin. "Whoever wishes to receive Christ in Eucharistic communion must be in the state of grace. If someone is conscious of having sinned mortally, he must not approach the Eucharist without having *first* received absolution in the Sacrament of Penance" (emphasis added) (1415). The catechism, of course, underscores the importance of frequent and even daily Communion for those who are properly disposed (1389). While acknowledging the divergence of liturgical traditions between East and West on the question of both species, the catechism nevertheless stresses that reception under one species still enables one "to receive the whole fruit of grace of the Eucharist" (1390), obviously dealing with some recent assertions that this is not the case.

Fruits of the Eucharist

And what are the fruits of a worthy reception of this most august Sacrament? "The principal fruit [is] intimate union with Christ Jesus," a union that "preserves, increases and renews the life of grace received in Baptism" (1391-92). Eucharistic communion also deepens one's life of charity, removes venial sins, and "preserves us from future mortal sins" (1393-95). Turning our gaze from heaven (always the first priority) to earth (which naturally and necessarily follows), the catechism then considers some horizontal results of Holy Communion: strengthening of ecclesial bonds, action on behalf of the poor, movement toward unity among separated Christians (1396-98). On this last matter, however, the catechism repeats the important cautions on Eucharistic sharing developed at Vatican II and in subsequent legislation, lest a unity that does not truly exist be precipitously presumed, to the detriment of real union in God's own time-frame.

Finally, we are told that the Eucharist should provide us with a perspective and focus that makes us long for heaven and ultimately leads us there. And so, we make our own the prayer of the ancient *Didache*: "May your grace come and this world pass" (1403). In and through the Eucharist does the grace of Christ come in the most significant way, preparing us for the day when this world does pass away and we are taken up into glory of the heavenly Banquet, which knows no end.

PENANCE

The introduction to the "The Sacraments of Healing" is so good that the best service to be provided here is simply to quote it.

"Through the sacraments of Christian initiation, man receives the new life of Christ. Now we carry this life 'in earthen vessels,' and it remains 'hidden with Christ in God.' We are still in our 'earthly tent,' subject to suffering, illness, and death. This new life as a child of God can be weakened and even lost by sin" (1420).

"The Lord Jesus Christ, physician of our souls and bodies, who forgave the sins of the paralytic and restored him to bodily health, has willed that his Church continue, in the power of the Holy Spirit, his work of healing and salvation, even among her own members. This is the purpose of the two sacraments of healing: the sacrament of Penance and the sacrament of Anointing of the Sick" (1421).

It is this first, the sacrament of Penace, that will occupy us in the present chapter.

Why a Distinct Sacrament of Penance?

After listing the several names historically accorded this sacrament, the catechism asks the fundamental question: "Why a Sacrament of Reconciliation after Baptism?" The obvious response is that man sins even after Baptism due to that "frailty and weakness of human nature," with "the inclination to sin," traditionally identified as "concupiscence." This "struggle of Christian life" against the forces of evil is assisted "[by] the grace of Christ." This process is "[that] of *conversion* directed toward holiness and eternal life to which the Lord never ceases to call us" (1425-26). Conversion, then, contrary to the Fundamentalists' view, is not a one-shot deal; it is a life-long journey that involves both God and the Church. Holding a resurging neo-Pelagianism at bay, the catechism warns that this effort "is not just a human work" but is preeminently a movement of that grace that enables one to "respond to the merciful love of God who loved us first" (1428). Secondly, conversion is in truth the work of the whole Church. As St. Ambrose put it, in the

Church, "there are water and tears: the water of Baptism and the tears of repentance" (1429).

The section on "Interior Penance" contains many salutary reminders, like the following: " . . . Jesus' call to conversion and penance, like that of the prophets before him, does not aim first at outward works . . . but at the *conversion of the heart, interior conversion.* Without this, such penances remain sterile and false; however, interior conversion urges expression in visible signs, gestures and works of penance" (1430). But just what is this "interior repentance"? Nothing less than "a radical reorientation of our whole life, a return, a conversion to God with all our heart, an end of sin, a turning away from evil, with repugnance toward the evil actions we have committed." That's quite a mouthful, but there's even more: " . . . the desire and resolution to change one's life, with hope in God's mercy and trust in the help of his grace" (1431). For the third time, we shall again read that all this happens as "a work of the grace" (1432), lest we think we can do this on our own or, equally important, lest we look at the immensity of the task and despair of its accomplishment. The following paragraph also recalls the fact that since the first Easter this work of conversion under the impulse of grace is, in a special way, the work of the Holy Spirit.

Next are given the three traditional forms of penance: fasting, prayer and almsgiving. These form a unity, for "taking up one's cross each day and following Jesus is the surest way of penance." All this is rooted in the nourishment that comes from the Eucharist, for "it is a remedy to free us from our daily faults and to preserve us from mortal sins" (1434-36).

With the context properly set, one can now appropriately discuss the sacrament itself. Although every sin "is before all else an offense against God, a rupture of communion with him," it also has an ecclesial dimension that calls for a liturgical act to deal with it (1440). Clearly, it is "only God [who] forgives sins," but it is likewise true that "he gives this power to men to exercise in his name." Why? "Christ has willed that in her prayer and life and action his whole Church should be the sign and instrument of the forgiveness and reconciliation that he acquired for us at the price of his blood," confiding "[this] power of absolution to the apostolic ministry" (1441-42). This communal aspect of forgiveness is well expressed by reference to the action of Christ himself who, it is good to remember, "not only forgave sins," but also "reintegrated forgiven sinners into the community of the People of God" (1443). In handling the scriptural basis for the sacrament, as one might expect, Matthew 16 is treated, with a most helpful explanation of the power of the keys (1445), as a fitting preface to a brief historical overview of the various forms this sacrament has taken down the centuries, albeit with a consistent and fundamental structure (1446-49).

Constituent Elements of the Sacrament

The primary component of Penance is contrition, which is "[a] sorrow of the soul and detestation for the sin committed, together with the resolution not to sin again" (1451). It may be "perfect" (that is, springing solely from the love of God Who has been injured by the sin) or "imperfect" (stemming from more human motives, like fear of eternal punishment in hell) (1452-53).

The text observes that "confession to a priest is an essential part of the sacrament of Penance," which is required to be received "at least once a year" when one is conscious of grave sins. Cautions are levelled about the necessity of this sacrament: "Anyone who is aware of having committed a mortal sin must not receive Holy Communion, even if he experiences deep contrition, without having first received sacramental absolution. . . . Children must go to the sacrament of Penance before receiving Holy Communion for the first time" (1456-57); this advice needs to become part of the normal catechetical training and pastoral practice of the Church in the United States once again. The catechism also encourages "the regular confession of our venial sins" since "[it] helps us form our conscience, fight against evil tendencies, lets ourselves be healed by Christ and progress in the life of the Spirit" (1458).

Confessing is not enough; satisfaction must also be made. Thus "the confessor proposes the performance of certain acts of 'satisfaction' or 'penance' to be performed by the penitent in order to repair the harm caused by sin and to re-establish habits befitting a disciple of Christ" (1494). "Only [those] priests who have received the faculty of absolving from the authority of the Church can forgive sins in the name of Christ" (1495), embodying within themselves the qualities of the Good Shepherd, the Good Samaritan, the merciful father of the prodigal son, and the just but merciful judge of the parable. A good confessor needs to have knowledge of both human and divine affairs; "he must love the truth, be faithful to the Magisterium of the Church, and lead the penitent with patience toward healing and full maturity." Likewise, he must be a man of prayer and penance himself. The seriousness of the seal of confession is given due consideration as well (1465-67).

Fruits of Penance

The effects of this wonderful sacrament are many: "reconciliation with God by which the penitent recovers grace; reconciliation with the Church; remission of the eternal punishment incurred by mortal sins; remission, at least in part, of temporal punishments resulting from sin; peace and serenity of conscience, and spiritual consolation; an increase of spiritual strength for the Christian battle" (1496). Such an impressive array of benefits should lead anyone to deepen one's appreciation for this sacrament and to inspire one to use it with regularity and devotion. A final point is made that "individual and integral confession of grave sins followed by absolution remains the only ordinary means of reconciliation with God and with the Church" (1497).

In the next place we find a presentation on the Catholic doctrine of indulgences, which "are closely linked to the effects of the sacrament of Penance." The traditional definition is offered as "a remission before God of the temporal punishment due to sins whose guilt has already been forgiven." It may be "partial" or "plenary," and "may be applied to the living or the dead." Indulgences touch on personal responsibility, the everlasting bonds within the communion of saints, participation in the process of one's own salvation (1471).

Finally, we are brought through the liturgical rite itself. Much emphasis is placed on the importance of individual confession and absolution due, no doubt, to abuses of general absolution (1483-84). In a more positive light, this discipline of the Church is presented as an element of the personalism demonstrated in the forgiving ministry exercised by the Lord himself during his sojourn on earth. "Personal confession is thus the form most expressive of reconciliation with God and with the Church" (1484). If confessors and penitents alike took this counsel to heart, the face of the Church and the earth itself could easily be renewed.

HOLY ORDERS

The treatment of the Sacrament of Orders begins with the

reminder that this is "the sacrament of apostolic ministry," conferred in three degrees: episcopate, presbyterate, diaconate; the first two orders are a ministerial participation in the priesthood of Christ while the last is intended to assist and serve the first two (1536-50). The word "presbyterate" is used here, as well as in the ordination rite, to distinguish the priesthood of the presbyter from that of the bishop; when the ministry they hold in common is intended (e.g., offering the Eucharistic Sacrifice), "priesthood" is used.

Why is this sacrament called by the name it has? The word "Order," in Roman antiquity, designated a body of people constituted to fulfill a particular purpose, especially governance; "ordination" signifies incorporation into an "order." From the earliest days (within the New Testament itself), the Church has utilized that structure for divine objectives.

A brief overview of the history of the sacrament in the economy of salvation is given, starting with the tribe of Levi among the Chosen People. Very quickly, we are brought up to the "unique . . . priesthood of Christ," which serves as the model and pattern for all Christian priesthood. Some Fundamentalists, for example, express concern or even shock over talk about Christian priests other than Jesus Christ. This is to misunderstand the nature of Christ's communication of his power and authority to the apostles and their successors. At the same time, with St. Thomas Aquinas we realize that in the strictest sense, "Christ is the true priest, the others being only his ministers" (1544-45).

Ordained Priests among a Priestly People

In point of fact, all Christians share in the priesthood of the Lord through Baptism, so that the entire People of God is a priestly people; there are, however, certain men taken from among the body of the faithful to participate in Christ's priesthood in a special manner. Thus it is that the Church speaks of the ordained priest as one who "acts in *persona Christi Capitis* [in the person of Christ the Head]. . . . Through the ordained ministry, especially that of bishops and priests, the presence of Christ as head of the Church is made visible in the midst of the community of believers" (1548-49).

As lofty as all this is, the catechism also realistically notes that the grace of the Holy Spirit "does not guarantee all acts of ministers in the same way." In fact, the sinfulness of the ordained can have the effect of diminishing "the apostolic fruitfulness of the Church" (1550). The text goes on to stress that "the priesthood is ministerial," that is, it is "a [true] *service.*" Furthermore, "it depends entirely on Christ and on his unique priesthood . . . The sacrament of Holy Orders communicates a 'sacred power' which is none other than that of Christ" (1551).

The priest represents Christ to the Church and equally the Church to God. That should not be misunderstood to mean, however, that "priests are the delegates of the community," for they are always and everywhere first of all the representatives of Christ. "It is because the ministerial priesthood represents Christ that it can represent the Church" (1553).

The episcopate is given full consideration, relying heavily on Vatican II, which did so much to put as fine a face on this ministry as Vatican I did with the papacy. Hence, we read that "bishops, in an eminent and visible manner, take the place of Christ himself, teacher, shepherd and priest" (1558). The point is made that "the lawful ordination of a bishop requires a special intervention of the Bishop of Rome, because he is the supreme visible bond of the communion of the particular Churches in the one Church and the guarantor of their freedom" (1559). At the same time, this theology of *communio* de-

mands that bishops be concerned for the good of the entire
Church, and not simply the local church over which they preside. The bishop embodies ecclesial unity in a singular way,
which comes across particularly when he celebrates the Eucharist; in that moment, it "has a quite special significance as
an expression of the Church gathered around the altar, with
the one who represents Christ, the Good Shepherd and Head
of his Church" (1561).

The second rank of ordained ministers is that of presbyters,
"*co-workers of the episcopal order*, for the proper fulfillment of
the apostolic mission that had been entrusted to it by Christ"
(1562). With the bishops, presbyters build, sanctify and govern Christ's Body, his Church. In this work, priests "depend on
the bishops," with whom they share "their sacerdotal dignity."
Priests "are consecrated in order to preach the Gospel and shepherd the faithful as well as to celebrate divine worship as *true
priests of the New Testament*" (1564). They are never more
priests than in the celebration of the Eucharist; beyond that,
"from this unique sacrifice, their whole priestly ministry draws
its strength" (1566).

Great emphasis is laid on the unity of bishops and priests,
who together form a sole *presbyterium* with diverse functions.
The promise of obedience to the bishop made at ordination
and the bishop's kiss of peace have important and on-going
implications, for in the latter is signified that "the bishop considers them [the priests] his co-workers, his sons, his brothers
and his friends, and that they in return owe him love and obedience." The unity of the priesthood is also highlighted when
all priests attending an ordination join the bishop in imposing
hands on the ordinands. (1567-68)

Deacons are ordained, with only the bishop imposing hands
to denote their special attachment to him "in the tasks of his

'diakonia' [service]." The functions of a deacon are outlined, and mention is made of the reinstitution of this ministry as a permanent order in the Latin Rite (the East had always kept it so) at the Second Vatican Council (1569-71).

The Rite, Minister, Candidates and Effects of the Sacrament

Moving on to the liturgical celebration of the sacrament, the catechism observes that, whenever possible, it should be administered on a Sunday, in the cathedral church, with solemnity, in the midst of the Eucharist. "The *essential rite* of Holy Orders for all three degrees consists in the bishop's imposition of hands on the head of the ordinand and in the bishop's specific consecratory prayer asking God for the outpouring of the Holy Spirit and his gifts proper to the ministry to which the candidate is being ordained" (1573). For the ordination of priests and bishops, the anointing with chrism signifies the work of the Holy Spirit who will make fruitful the ordinand's ministry. A good explanation is given for the items conferred on the bishop during his ordination: ring, miter, crosier.

A bishop is the only possible minister of this sacrament. Regarding the recipient of the sacrament, we are told that "only a baptized man validly receives sacred ordination." The catechism says this is so because "the Church recognizes herself to be bound by this choice made by the Lord himself. For this reason the ordination of women is not possible" (1577). It continues to argue that "no one has a *right* to receive the Sacrament of Holy Orders" (emphasis in original), asserting that "no one claims this office for himself." On the contrary, one who perceives the call of God "must humbly submit his desire to the authority of the Church, who has the responsibility and right to call someone to receive orders." And most importantly, "like every grace this sacrament can be *received* only as an unmerited gift" (1578). Some discussion is offered on the charism of celibacy required for priesthood in the West, as well as the esteem in which it is held in the East, and on its necessity for all episcopal candidates in East and West alike (1579-80).

A sacramental, indelible character is conferred in Holy Orders, just as it is in Baptism and Confirmation. Answering those who press for a temporary commitment to priesthood, the catechism reminds us that this character "cannot be repeated or conferred temporarily" (1582). Granted, a man can be discharged from ministerial functions or can be enjoined from exercising them for a just cause, "but he cannot become a layman again in the strict sense" because "the character imprinted by ordination is for ever" (1583).

The section concludes with two salutary reminders in this day of a priestly identity crisis. St. John Vianney muses that "if we really understood the priest on earth, we would die not of fright but of love" (1589). Finally, St. Ignatius of Antioch taught eighteen centuries ago that so irreplaceable is the hierarchical constitution of the Church that "without the bishop, presbyters, and deacons, one cannot speak of the Church" (1593).

THE SACRAMENT OF MARRIAGE

Quoting the Code of Canon Law, the catechism begins its reflections on the Sacrament of Marriage in this manner: "The matrimonial covenant, by which a man and a woman establish between themselves a partnership of the whole of life, is by its nature ordered toward the good of the spouses and the procreation and education of offspring; this covenant between baptized persons has been raised by Christ the Lord to the dignity of a sacrament." That says it all, to be sure, but it also calls for a good deal of analysis.

Marriage in Human History

The catechism considers this sacrament in four stages as it has been experienced in history: in the order of creation, under the reign of sin, under the tutelage of the Law, and in the Lord.

From the beginning of creation, we are reminded, "the vocation to marriage is written in the very nature of man and woman as they came from the hand of the Creator." Indeed, this is bound up with creation itself, for "God who created man out of love also calls him to love—the fundamental and innate vocation of every human being." Beyond that, "man and woman were created for one another," and are each others' "equal[s]." As Genesis 2 puts it, this is the reason why a man leaves his parents and clings to his wife to become one flesh; this is the primordial understanding of marriage in the mind and plan of the Creator (1603-05).

But that is not reality as we experience, is it? Faith calls us to realize, however, that what we experience is not normal; in fact, it is a deformation of the original plan, occurring as a result of the entrance of sin into the world, which sin not only ruptured the relationship between God and man, but likewise did violence to all human relations, including that of marriage. Thus, Genesis teaches, the natural attraction of man and woman becomes a source of tension and even an occasion for self-assertion and domination (1606-68).

The good God did not abandon man to his own devices and so gave the Law that developed "[the] moral conscience concerning the unity and indissolubility of marriage." This led to the slow but sure repudiation of the polygamy practiced by patriarchs and kings. It is also good to recall that the Mosaic Law also had the effect of "protecting the wife from arbitrary domination by the husband" (1610). The prophets contributed mightily to growth in appreciation for the married state in seeing the covenant of God with Israel under the image of the exclusive and faithful love of marriage. That continued in works like the Books of Ruth, Tobit and the Song of Songs (1611-12).

Matrimony took a quantum leap forward with the coming of Christ. "The Church attaches great importance to Jesus' presence at the wedding at Cana. She sees in it the confirmation of the goodness of marriage and the proclamation that henceforth marriage will be an efficacious sign of Christ's presence." The goal of the Lord was to return the Chosen People to "the original meaning of the union of man and woman as the Creator willed it from the beginning," thus declaring marriage to be indissoluble in his powerful words: "What therefore God has joined together, let no man put asunder." Christ did not, however, impose a burden without also providing his assistance, which consists of both his grace and his own example of selfless love. St. Paul brought this a step further in his pronouncement that married life is a great "mystery" that refers to the union of Christ and his Church (Eph 5:31-2). In a most insightful passage, the catechism speaks of all Christian life being at root "a nuptial mystery" which we can see when we behold Baptism, "the nuptial bath which precedes the wedding feast, the Eucharist" (1613-17).

Nor does the text shy away from discussing the relationship between marriage and "virginity for the sake of the kingdom," making the point that the two "come from the Lord himself. It is he who gives them meaning and grants them the grace which is indispensable for living them out in conformity with his will." Citing St. John Chrysostom, it says, "Whoever denigrates marriage also diminishes the glory of virginity. Whoever praises it makes virginity more admirable and resplendent. [For in the final analysis] what appears good only in comparison with evil would not be truly good. The most excellent good is something even better than what is admitted to be good" (1618-20).

Requirements for a Christian Marriage

It is worth emphasizing that the catechism spends only four paragraphs on the wedding ceremony, not because it is unimportant but because none of that makes any sense unless everything else is in place; this is in sharp contrast to the way in which most American Catholics view marriage—with all the preparation for the big day and so little thought given to the rest of one's life together. The catechism speaks of the value of having the wedding take place in the context of the Eucharistic Sacrifice and of having prepared for the event by a worthy reception of the Sacrament of Penance. It also takes cognizance of the divergent but complementary views of West and East on the ministers of the sacrament (the spouses themselves in the former, the priest in the latter) (1621-24).

Much is rightly made of the matter of matrimonial consent that demands that the spouses be "free to contract marriage, who freely express their consent." In what does this freedom consist? "Not being under constraint; not impeded by any natural or ecclesiastical law" (1625). This is so key because "the Church holds the exchange of consent between the spouses to be *the indispensable element* that 'makes the marriage'" (emphasis added, 1626). By this consent, they "mutually give themselves to each other" (1627). "The priest (or deacon) who assists at the celebration of a marriage receives the consent of the spouses in the name of the Church and gives the blessing of the Church. The presence of the Church's minister (and also of the witnesses) visibly expresses the fact that marriage is an ecclesial reality" (1630). This "ecclesial reality" comes out through the celebration of a liturgical act, through the introduction of the couple into an "ecclesial *ordo*" (like the *ordo* of the priesthood), and by being perceived as "a state of life in the Church." Finally, "the public character of the consent protects the 'I do' once given and helps the spouses remain faithful to it" (1631).

The catechism zeroes in on the angle of fidelity by underscoring the significance of marriage preparation, which begins in the Christian home and is given impetus and direction by the Church's pastors.

A very realistic presentation is made of mixed marriages, with a distinction offered between one which involves a Catholic and another Christian and one between a Catholic and an unbaptized person. While observing that this difference in faith "does not constitute an insurmountable obstacle," it cautions that the dissimilarity "must not be underestimated." The text gives special attention to the union with an unbaptized person: "Differences about faith and the very notion of marriage, but also different religious mentalities, can become sources of tension in marriage, especially as regards the education of children. The temptation to religious indifference can then arise."

The catechism states that the expressed permission or dispensation of the Church for mixed marriages is required to ensure that "both parties know and do not exclude the essential ends and properties of marriage and the obligations assumed by the Catholic party concerning the baptism and education of the children in the Catholic Church." The text notes with pleasure that in certain countries it is now commonplace to provide ecumenical pastoral care for mixed marriages. It also challenges Catholics married to non-Christians to take as their particular task the sanctification of the other, in the hope that this will "lead to the free conversion of the other spouse to the Christian faith" (1633-37).

Effects of the Sacrament

What are the effects of the Sacrament of Marriage? "A *bond* between the spouses which by its very nature is perpetual and exclusive," which makes it then most like God's love. The permanence of marriage is seen as divine law, so that "the Church does not have the power to contravene this disposition of divine wisdom." To live this vocation, grace is needed. "This grace proper to the sacrament of Matrimony is intended to perfect the couple's love and to strengthen their indissoluble unity. By this grace they 'help one another to attain holiness in their married life and in welcoming and educating their children.'" Lest anyone be ignorant, we read that *"Christ is the source of this grace,"* which is why the demands of marriage are not too much to bear and loving with a supernatural, sensitive and fruitful love becomes entirely possible (1638-42).

A very detailed section on "The Goods and Requirements of Conjugal Love" follows, restating traditional teaching on the indissolubility of marriage, the necessity of absolute fidelity, and the need for openness to human life. The treatment of divorce and remarriage is compassionate, all the while reiterating the impossibility of receiving the sacraments while in an invalid second union (1643-50). Given the contraceptive mood in society-at-large and even in certain quarters of the Church, one should refer to the Commandments section of the catechism for a discussion of this matter, with special consideration given to *Humanae Vitae* of Pope Paul VI and *Familiaris Consortio* of Pope John Paul II.

Looking over the centuries, the catechism asserts that believing families were islands of Christian life in an unbelieving world, and so were rightly dubbed by Vatican II as domestic Churches, for "the home is [thus] the first school of Christian life and 'a school for human enrichment'" (1655-57). The text also mentions those who do not marry for a variety of reasons and asks all to remember that they too have a right to have a family, especially in the person of the Church.

And so, the Church concludes her teaching on that sacrament which makes possible all human society but also the divine society of the Church. In this connection, it is not inappropriate to recall an anecdote from the life of Pope St. Pius X who, with great pride, showed off his episcopal ring to his mother after his consecration. Evincing a very basic approach to life, she remarked that were it not for her wedding ring he would never have his bishop's ring!

ANOINTING OF THE SICK

Before launching into a discussion of the Sacrament of the Anointing of the Sick, itself, the catechism offers a superb analysis of the place of sickness in human life.

Sickness and Suffering for a Believer

Noting the potential consequences for an individual when faced with personal suffering, it observes that "illness can lead to anguish, self-absorption, sometimes even despair and revolt against God." It goes on, however, to highlight another possible effect: "It can also make a person more mature, helping him discern in his life what is not essential so that he can turn toward that which is." And, most importantly, "very often illness provokes a search for God and a return to him" (1501). The first set of responses to suffering is all too common today, leading people to turn to Dr. Death instead of God; it is the task of the Church to make sure that her sons and daughters see the values inherent in the second set and act accordingly.

Taking account of the general Old Testament understanding of suffering as punishment for sin, the text also reminds readers that even in the Hebrew Scriptures, especially with sacred authors like Deutero-Isaiah, "suffering can also have a redemptive meaning for the sins of others" (1502). Jesus, as the Suffering Servant of God prophesied of old, "has come to heal the whole man, soul and body;" indeed, "His compassion toward all who suffer goes so far that he identifies himself with them: 'I was sick and you visited me'" (Mt 25:36). But that concern of the Lord was not limited to his earthly life and ministry; it continues in and through the concerted efforts of his disciples in every age to alleviate suffering, wherever and whenever possible (1503).

In studying Christ's means of curing people, one can see how he utilized signs like saliva, imposition of hands, mud and cleansing actions and how the sick sought to touch him because of the power which emanated from his sacred Person. In the same way, he carries on his healing ministry in the Church in the sacraments, by which the Lord "continues to 'touch' us in order to heal us" (1504).

Why did Jesus not cure all the ills of the human family when he lived and walked among us? The catechism provides a critically important answer: "His healings were signs of the coming of the Kingdom of God. They announced a *more radical* healing: the victory over sin and death through his Passover" (emphasis added, 1505). This insight cannot be overemphasized since it deals with a perennial question, "If God is almighty and all-good, why doesn't he eliminate all suffering from the face of the earth?" The response calls us to seek to understand the ways of God, whereby he would have us lift our sights from the merely temporal to the eternal.

If our focus is limited to this world, the question is damning for God; if our eyes are set on something more and better, then we can begin to appreciate what is being said here. Some years ago in celebrating a funeral Mass for an AIDS victim, I reminded the congregation, to their amazement, that dying of AIDS was not the worst thing that could have happened to their friend; dying in the state of mortal sin was and, thank God, he had had the grace of repentance and many weeks of a full life in Christ before the Lord took him to himself. In so thoroughly a secular environment that we inhabit, the Church's teachings on suffering and death need constant restatement and reinforcement.

A Special Sacrament

A powerful way in which the Church does that is through her ministry to the sick, particularly in the sacrament which exists with them in mind. In tracing the history of the sacrament from the first evidence in the Epistle of James (1526), the catechism admits that as the centuries went on, increasingly the Anointing of the Sick was restricted to the dying, hence, its preconciliar name of "Extreme Unction" (that is, Last Anointing). That approach was changed, however, at the Second Vatican Council, which wished that the older and more original nature of the sacrament be restored (1512-13).

1. *Who should be anointed?* "The proper time for receiving this holy anointing has certainly arrived when the believer begins to be in danger of death because of illness or old age." Furthermore, "each time a Christian falls seriously ill, he may receive the Anointing of the Sick, and also when, after he has received it, the illness worsens" (1528-29). Therefore, the sacrament is no longer envisioned as reserved for those *in extremis*. At the same time, it is not to be used in a frivolous manner for routine maladies or less-than-serious (even if not necessarily life-threatening) illnesses.

2. *Who may anoint?* Again, following the apostolic tradition begun in the Epistle of James, we hold that "only priests. . . are ministers of the Anointing of the Sick" (1516); this needs to be understood in these days of so much pastoral confusion over ministry to the sick as not a few religious or laity insist that they who tend to the day-to-day spiritual needs of a patient have a right to administer this sacrament. The Church disagrees in the clearest of terms. What is the work of the non-ordained members of Christ's Body? It is their privilege and obligation to prepare the sick "to receive it [the sacrament] with good dispositions" and to assist the sick with "their prayers and fraternal attention" (1516).

3. *How is the sacrament celebrated?* Repeating what should be obvious but not always comprehended, this sacrament (precisely because it is a sacrament) "is a liturgical and communal celebration"; it "takes place in the family home, a hospital or church"; it may be done "for a single sick person or for a whole group of sick persons." It is most appropriate "to celebrate it within the Eucharist, the memorial of the Lord's Passover." When a Mass is not possible, it is good that this sacrament "be preceded by the sacrament of Penance and followed by the sacrament of the Eucharist." Of course, for those who are dying, this reception of Holy Communion is one's "viaticum," the food for one's final journey—into eternity (1517).

The sacramental rite calls for the proclamation of God's holy Word and for the special sign of this sacrament which is "the anointing of the forehead and hands of the sick person (in the Roman rite) or of other parts of the body (in the Eastern rite)"; this anointing with oil (blessed if possible by the bishop) is "accompanied by the liturgical prayer of the celebrant asking for the special grace of this sacrament" (1531).

4. *And what are the effects or graces flowing from a worthy*

reception?

They are manifold. "The uniting of the sick person to the passion of Christ, for his own good and that of the whole Church; the strengthening, peace, and courage to endure in a Christian manner the sufferings of illness or old age; the forgiveness of sins, if the sick person was not able to obtain it through the sacrament of Penance; the restoration of health, if it is conducive to the salvation of his soul; the preparation for passing over to eternal life" (1532). While all the benefits are valuable, in our time of diminished appreciation of the place of suffering, the grace to endure pain and discomfort for the good of others may be most crucial since it reminds the sick person of a sense of purpose and of having a place within the communion of saints, wherein one is assured of the prayers and support of the whole Church and in turn suffers with Christ for the good of all and out of love. This allows one to claim the sanctification that is rightfully that of a Christian and at the same time to increase the sanctification of others. If this notion were more firmly in place, it is doubtful that suffering and death would be the source of anxiety and even desperation which they are for so many in our society, with a regrettable number of Christians in that number as well.

OTHER LITURGICAL CELEBRATIONS
Sacramentals

Sacramentals are distinguished from sacraments in that the former have the Church as their author, while the latter are grounded in the intentions and acts of Christ himself. Sacramentals are important for many reasons, among them being those cited by Vatican II's *Sacrosanctum Concilium*: "By them men are disposed to receive the chief effect of the sacraments, and various occasions in life are rendered holy" (1667).

What constitutes a sacramental? "They always include a prayer, often accompanied by a specific sign, such as the laying on of hands, the sign of the cross, or the sprinkling of holy water (which recalls Baptism)" (1668). We are made to remember that sacramentals do not confer grace in the same manner as the sacraments; rather, their use makes us ready to receive grace and to cooperate with it. Inasmuch as the Incarnation is the principal dogma of our faith, it is logical that Catholics should not shy away from the use of created, material realities as means of putting us in touch with uncreated, spiritual realities.

"*Blessings* (of persons, meals, objects, and places) come first" among sacramentals (1671). Sometimes these blessings involve the consecration of a person (e.g., virgins, abbots or abbesses, lectors, acolytes) or of objects destined for divine worship (e.g., a church building, altar, bells, vestments, vessels). The catechism also mentions the rite of exorcism as an example here, noting both the value of exorcism and the caution the Church exercises in the use of this ceremony (1673).

In treating matters like the veneration of relics, pilgrimages and the like, the text praises the many forms of popular piety, but also is careful to call for their incorporation into the broader picture of Catholic worship, insisting that all such things should be inspired by good theology and a healthy relationship to the liturgy proper (1676).

Christian Funerals

In concluding the worship component of the catechism, the text calls to mind for us that "all the sacraments, and principally those of Christian initiation, have as their goal the last Passover of the child of God which, through death, leads him into the life of the Kingdom" (1680). That leads into the rituals of the Church that facilitate the final passage into eternity.

In equally pastoral and theological fashion, we are made to see how the Sacraments of Baptism and Holy Eucharist truly reach their fulfillment in the Rite of Christian Burial. In a touching passage, we read, "The Church who, as Mother, has borne the Christian sacramentally in her womb during his earthly pilgrimage, accompanies him at his journey's end, in order to surrender him 'into the Father's hands.' She offers to the Father, in Christ, the child of his grace, and she commits to the earth, in hope, the seed of the body that will rise in glory" (1683).

DISCUSSION QUESTIONS

Section One: The Sacramental Economy

1. Explain the significance of Christ's sending the Holy Spirit to the Apostles in respect to the Church's liturgy.

2. What is the role of the Holy Spirit in the liturgy?

3. Why must we receive the sacraments with the proper disposition?

4. What three sacraments can only be received once? Why is this so?

5. How is sacramental life beneficial to the individual believer and to the Church?

6. Who celebrates the liturgy?

7. What purposes do sacred images serve?

8. Why is Sunday, "the day of the Lord," the principal day of the celebration of the Eucharist?

9. Explain the importance of remembering Mary and the other saints in the liturgy.

10. Who should celebrate the Liturgy of the Hours? Why?

Section Two: The Seven Sacraments of the Church

Baptism

11. Tell why Baptism is the foundation of Christian life.

A TOUR OF THE CATHOLIC CATECHISM

12. How does the symbol of water explain the meaning of Baptism?

13. What are the elements of the baptismal rite?

14. Who can receive Baptism?

15. Who can baptize?

16. In case of an "emergency baptism," what two elements must be present?

17. What is meant when we say that God himself is not "bound to the sacraments"?

18. What are the rights and responsibilities of the baptized?

Confirmation
19. Why is the reception of Confirmation essential for the completion of baptismal grace?

20. What does the name "Christian" mean?

21. How do the Eastern and Western rites of Confirmation differ? What are the advantages of each?

22. In the rite of Confirmation, what do the anointing with chrism, imposition of hands, and kiss of peace signify?

23. Why is Confirmation so important?

24. Who can receive the Sacrament of Confirmation?

25. What should be the thrust of catechesis for Confirmation?

26. What is a sponsor's function?

The Eucharist
27. What are the various names for the Eucharist?

28. What two parts of the Mass form its basic structure?

29. Who may preside over the Mass?

30. When does the Eucharistic presence of Christ begin and end?

31. Why is the Eucharist the most perfect form of worship?

32. Why is there intercessory prayer within the Eucharistic prayer?

33. Explain transubstantiation.

34. What does the altar represent?

35. Who can receive Communion?

36. What are the effects of receiving the Eucharist?

Penance
37. What is the purpose of Penance and Anointing of the Sick, the two sacraments of healing?

38. Why do Catholics believe conversion to be a life-long process?

39. What is meant by "interior" penance?

40. Name the three traditional forms of penance.

41. Define contrition. What are perfect and imperfect contrition?

42. Is personal confession to a priest necessary? Explain.

43. Why must we expiate, or do penance, for our sins?

44. Who has the power to forgive sins?

45. What are the spiritual effects of Penance?

46. What are indulgences? To whom may indulgences be applied?

The Anointing of the Sick
47. What was the deeper significance of Jesus' cures when he lived among us?

48. When should someone be anointed?

49. Who may anoint the sick?

50. What is the responsibility of the laity in assisting the sick?

51. What should the celebration of the Anointing of the Sick include?

52. Define viaticum.

53. What are the effects of celebrating the sacrament of Anointing of the Sick?

54. What should be the place of suffering in Christian life?

Holy Orders
55. Why is this sacrament called "Orders"?

56. Name the three degrees conferred in the Sacrament of Orders.

57. Explain what is meant when we say the priest acts *in persona Christi Capitis*?

58. What are the functions of a bishop?

59. What are the functions of a presbyter (priest)?

60. In what ways is the unity of the priesthood made evident?

61. What are the functions of a deacon?

62. State the two elements that are necessary in the rite of ordination for bishops, presbyters and deacons.

63. Who can be ordained? Why is this so?

64. Why is ordination permanent?

Marriage
65. What is the significance of the matrimonial covenant?

66. Trace marriage as it has been experienced through four stages in history.

67. How are marriage and "virginity for the kingdom" related?

68. What is the indispensable element that makes a marriage?

69. Why should a marriage celebration be within the framework of a liturgical celebration, before a priest or deacon and other witnesses?

70. What are some difficulties that may arise from a mixed marriage?

71. What are the effects of the Sacrament of Matrimony?

72. What is required of conjugal love?

73. Why is the family called "the domestic Church"?

part three:
LIFE IN CHRIST

*Man is the only creature on earth that God
has willed for its own sake . . .*
Gaudium et Spes

part three:
LIFE IN CHRIST

S ome observers of the order of things in the catechism will express surprise that the section devoted to Christian morality comes so late in the game, but its placement is not accidental or haphazard. Morality can only be integrated and lived when put in the proper framework. According to traditional Christian thinking, moral living flows from a correct understanding of doctrine; secondly, morality is possible only under the impulse of divine grace, which comes to us preeminently through the Church's sacramental system.

"Life in Christ" begins with an excerpt of Pope St. Leo the Great's magnificent Christmas homily: "Christian, recognize your dignity and, now that you share in God's own nature, do not return to your former base condition by sinning. Remember who is your head and of whose body you are a member. Never forget that you have been rescued from the power of darkness and brought into the light of the Kingdom of God" (1691). That is the necessary context for undertaking the demands of a Gospel life. If believers truly understood their incredible dignity, they would never diminish or even destroy it by sinful acts or patterns of behavior. And so, it is quite right to maintain that the first and most necessary step in assisting people of any age to conform their lives to that of Christ is convincing them of the nearly unspeakable identity which is theirs, thanks to God's favor and grace.

The fundamental reality making Christian morality do-able is one's Baptism, whereby Christians die to sin and are made alive to God in Christ Jesus, thus "participat[ing] in the life of the Risen Lord" (1694). In other words, we do not accomplish this noble task on our own steam; rather, we are given the energy, strength and dynamism of the Spirit of Christ, so that what is clearly impossible for unaided human beings becomes feasible for the simple reason that nothing is impossible for God. From the tenderest age, disciples of the Lord are offered a choice between two mutually exclusive "ways": the way of the Lord Jesus, leading to fullness of life, and the way of the world, leading to destruction.

Instruction in Christian morality is, according to the catechism, a multi-faceted thing. It should be, we are told, a catechesis of the Holy Spirit ("the interior Master of life" who "inspires, guides, corrects and strengthens"); grace (that saves us at the outset and makes our efforts fruitful); the beatitudes (Christ's "way" in a unique and singular manner); sin and forgiveness (recognizing the truth of oneself as a sinner and simultaneously as one offered God's merciful love); human virtues; Christian virtues; and the two-fold commandment of charity. Finally, moral instruction should always be *"an ecclesial catechesis,"* that is, coming to the conclusion that it is essentially through the Church "that Christian life can grow, develop, and be communicated" (1697).

The catechism stresses the need for Christian morality to be grounded in a relationship with Jesus Christ, who described himself as "the way, and the truth, and the life" (Jn 14:6). All too often, in our recent past, catechesis told youngsters and adults alike what should be done but seemed to omit the relational element, which undergirds everything, making sense of it all. Jesus does not give us abstract norms of life or a Herculean moral code. He gives us the Law, to be sure, but he also gives us himself as both the example for living that Law and the strength to do so. We are not alone in trying to live up to the demands of the Gospel; Jesus is with us through it all.

SECTION ONE: MAN'S VOCATION: LIFE IN THE SPIRIT

In this first section of "Life in Christ," the authors of the catechism sketch out the basis for the vocation of man and locate it, once more, in the dignity of the human person. Topics coming under that rubric include: man as the image of God; the meaning of beatitude and freedom; moral acts and human passions; the formation of conscience; the development of virtues. Someone anxious to "cut to the chase" might well ask, "Where does sin fit into the picture?" It is the very last element treated—and rightly so. All too often in what would pass for "traditional" catechesis, preachers and teachers began with sin—and generally ended there. But that is a very truncated, superficial, incomplete and misleading method of instruction. The catechism takes the longer way around, but the only one that can assure us of appropriate results, namely, life in the Spirit.

Man in the Image of God

And so, we begin where God began: man created in the divine image and likeness. Of course, we know that man disfigured that correspondence between the divine and the human, however, God came to the rescue in Christ, so that it "has been restored to its original beauty and ennobled by the grace of God" (1701). In the beginning, God constituted the first man and woman in perfect holiness and harmony and "endowed [them] with 'a spiritual and immortal soul.'" This concern for man was such that the Fathers of Vatican II in *Gaudium et Spes* could declare that "'the only creature on earth that God has willed for its own sake'" was man. Not surprisingly, then, do we learn that "from his conception, he [man] is destined for eternal beatitude," participating even now "in the light and power of the divine Spirit" (1703-04). The gift of free will, the ability to choose between good and evil, is a primary datum in appreciating human dignity, while "living a moral life bears witness" to the same (1706).

Truth be told, however, we know that the proper use of free will is not an easy thing. Martin Luther would go so far as to say that the original fall from grace was so precipitous and catastrophic that the human person is and always will be incapable of any good. The Church at the Reformation and ever since, however, disagreed with the pessimistic Luther; her view is more optimistic, or better, realistic. Hence, she holds a position that takes into account human experience, common sense and divine revelation: Man "still desires the good, but his nature bears the wound of original sin. He is now inclined to evil and subject to error" (1707).

And finally, Christ's saving passion delivers us from the clutches of Satan and restores us to friendship with God in the Spirit. Therefore, anyone who believes in Christ has renewed access to the Father, becoming "a son of God." With what effect? "This filial adoption transforms him by giving him the ability to follow the example of Christ. It makes him capable of acting rightly and doing good," so that under the influence of grace, "the moral life blossoms into eternal life in the glory of heaven" (1709).

The Vocation to Beatitude

Just what is this "eternal life in the glory of heaven" (1709)? It is the experience of beatitude, which one finds spelled out in the so-called "Eight Beatitudes" as recorded by St. Matthew; they form "the heart of Jesus' preaching . . . depict the countenance of Jesus Christ and portray His charity." At the same time, these counter-cultural and "paradoxical promises" also "express the vocation of the faithful" and "sustain hope in the midst of tribulations" (1716-17).

Have we yet discovered what "beatitude" is, in itself? Not quite. We read that "the Beatitudes respond to the natural desire for happiness" (1718). Hapless translations of Greek and Latin texts have informed us that "beatitude" is the equivalent of "happiness," but we can see that the catechism is aiming at something rather different. Beatitude has a relationship to "the (natural) desire for happiness," but it is much, much more, for it "surpasses the understanding and powers of man" and "comes from an entirely free gift of God" (1722). Whereas happiness can be a very ephemeral and shallow thing, beatitude is connected to such profound and authentic affairs as "the coming of the Kingdom of God," "the vision of God," "entering into the joy of the Lord," "entering into God's rest." In case the picture is still not focused, beatitude is further defined as making us "partakers of the divine nature" and bringing us "into the glory of Christ and into the joy of the Trinitarian life" (1720-21). This appealing and inviting prospect, however, is not doled out, willy-nilly, by some divine Candy Man. On the contrary, "the beatitude we are promised confronts us with decisive moral choices," calling us to tread "the paths that lead to the Kingdom of heaven . . . by everyday acts" (1723-24).

Human Freedom

It is curious that an age like ours that so exalts and even exaggerates human freedom would have so low an estimate of human responsibility. The Church, on the other hand, as Mother and Teacher of the human family for two millennia, links the two: "Freedom makes man *responsible* for his acts to the extent that they are voluntary. Progress in virtue, knowledge of the good, and ascesis enhance the mastery of the will over its acts" (1734). Furthermore, every human "has the natural right to be recognized as a free and responsible being" (1738). Although we know that "*imputability* and responsibility for an action can be diminished or even nullified by ignorance, inadvertence, duress, fear, habit, inordinate attachments, and other psychological or social factors" (1735), we do nothing for human dignity by taking these exceptional instances as normative, thus reducing the human person to a helpless and totally conditioned organism.

The proper exercise of freedom today is mightily influenced by the yesterdays of its misuse throughout our history; the first error or "alienation engendered a multitude of others" (1739). Many contemporary folks show themselves to be the true descendants of Adam and Eve when they claim a role for freedom in human activity that is essentially unrestricted and more accurately labeled "license." With good reason, therefore, does the text remind all that "the exercise of freedom does not imply a right to say or do everything," so that no concern is evidenced for "the economic, social, political, and cultural" ramifications of one's actions. The misuse of freedom has deep and lasting effects as man "becomes imprisoned within himself, disrupts neighborly fellowship, and rebels against divine truth"

PART THREE: LIFE IN CHRIST

(1740). Who cannot see in that description the modern situation?

The Christian understanding of freedom is inextricably united to truth that, as the Lord teaches, makes us truly free (cf. Jn 8:32). Beyond that, we believe that human freedom is best used in response to the movements of divine grace, for grace "is not in the slightest way a rival of our freedom when this freedom accords with the sense of the true and the good that God has put in the human heart." In point of fact, "the more docile we are to the promptings of grace, the more we grow in inner freedom and confidence during trials, such as those we face in the pressures and constraints of the outer world" (1742). This is so because grace orders our judgment to consider options from a divine perspective, and the closer our judgments come to God's, the more fully human they are as well.

The Morality of Human Acts

The first line of this section sets the tone: "Freedom makes man a moral subject." What does that mean? Very simply, that if one were not free, there could never be a discussion of right and wrong. Dogs and cats do not have courts of law or jails, precisely because they are not free beings. We can choose, thus making our acts capable of being "morally evaluated" as "either good or evil" (1749).

In determining such morality, we are guided by three considerations: the object chosen, the intention of the act and the circumstances. The starting point for moral discourse is the goodness of the object in view; if it is not good in itself, no amount of good will can alter it—"The end does not justify the means" (1753). Catholic morality has always operated within the poles of objectivity and subjectivity. While we find it plain to conclude that a good intention cannot make good an inherently evil act (the catechism lists offenses like blasphemy, perjury, murder and adultery), it is often forgotten that good acts can be rendered less good or even wrong due to a faulty intention (e.g., fasting or praying which are good in themselves but done to be seen by men). In sum, "a morally good act requires the goodness of its object, of its end, and of its circumstances together" (1760).

Passions

The average person hears the word "passion" and thinks of sexual desire, usually of a disordered nature. In reality, the passions are much more basic and neutral; they "are emotions or movements of the sensitive appetite that incline us to act or not to act in regard to something felt or imagined to be good or evil." Just as importantly, "they form the passageway and ensure the connection between the life of the senses and the life of the mind." As one might expect, then, "the most fundamental passion is love, aroused by the attraction of the good." St. Thomas Aquinas teaches that "to love is to will the good of another." And St. Augustine, who certainly knew the meaning of passion in every sense, reflects that passions "are evil if love is evil and good if it is good" (1763-66).

As should be clear by now, "in themselves passions are neither good nor evil. They are morally qualified only to the extent that they effectively engage reason and will." But for genuinely human activity to occur, it is necessary that "the passions be governed by reason." We do not belong to the lower regions of the animal kingdom in which instinct is the operative principle of behavior, whereby one is buffeted by "strong feelings" in a particular direction. Instead, "the upright will orders the movements of the senses it appropriates to the good and to beatitude; an evil will succumbs to disordered passions and exacerbates them." Regular, repeated action in the former manner produces virtues; regular, repeated action in the latter manner produces vices (1767-69).

This apprehension of human nature is then inserted into the perspective of faith when the text stresses that "the perfection of the moral good consists in man's being moved to the good not only by his will but also by his 'heart'" (1775), a heart that has been touched by Jesus Christ.

Conscience

When the average modern hears the word "conscience," he tends to equate it with opinion or personal position. The Church has a totally different understanding, one which is thoroughly objective. Quoting the Fathers of the Second Vatican Council, the catechism speaks of conscience as the source for man's discovery of "a law which he has not laid upon himself but which he must obey . . . a law inscribed by God . . . His conscience is man's most secret core and his sanctuary. There he is alone with God whose voice echoes in his depths" (1776). Reading on, we find that it is conscience that "enjoins (the human person) at the appropriate moment to do good and to avoid evil. It also judges particular choices, approving those that are good and denouncing those that are evil." Yet again, "it welcomes the commandments" (1777). This is a far cry from popular misconceptions of "conscience," which John Cardinal Newman dubs "the aboriginal Vicar of Christ" (1778).

Conscience is a kind of multi-phasic process which includes: apprehension of moral principles; application of them to practical circumstances; and judgment about concrete acts, either to be performed or already performed. This process enables one to act with responsibility. At times we hear people say that they can perform certain acts "in good conscience;" all too often that is because they are acting from deformed or dead consciences, leading us to ask how one's conscience can be properly formed—which is the only guarantee of true freedom and peace of soul. The catechism teaches that "in the formation of conscience the Word of God is the light for our path." Also indispensable is the examination of one's conscience "before the Lord's Cross" (1785). Furthermore, the gifts of the Holy Spirit, the advice and witness of others and the "authoritative teaching of the Church" are all guides as we move toward the goal of forming an "upright and truthful" conscience. Lest anyone imagine that this is an easy endeavor or a one-shot effort, we are reminded that this is, in truth, "a lifelong task" (1783-85).

We read that "a human being must always obey the certain judgment of his conscience." At the same time, we know that "it can happen that moral conscience remains in ignorance and makes erroneous judgments about acts to be performed or already committed" (1790). How can this happen? Once more, the Council Fathers are brought forth to explain that this occurs when people exert little effort at finding out the truth or when they are blinded to the truth by habitual sin. The catechism lists other sources for the break-down of the moral information system: ignorance of Christ and His Gospel; bad example; enslavement to passions; subscribing to a false notion of autonomy; rejection of the Magisterium and its teachings; and lack of genuine conversion. The resolution of the problem, then, resides in one's willingness to rout out the sources of misinformation, so as to allow the light of truth to shine within that personal sanctuary that is the human conscience.

The Virtues

While most people would rejoice to be called virtuous, most

would also be hard-pressed to define "virtue." At a human level, we can look upon virtues as "firm attitudes, stable dispositions, habitual perfections of intellect and will that govern our actions, order our passions, and guide our conduct according to reason and faith." One who is virtuous is capable of performing good acts repeatedly and with ease (1804).

First consideration is given to those virtues dubbed "cardinal" (Latin, *cardo*, hinge) because "[they] play a pivotal role" in the development of a moral life: prudence, justice, fortitude and temperance (1805). In quick succession, we learn the identity and purpose of each. *Prudence* helps us to perceive our true good and to choose the correct means for attaining it; *justice* is the determination to give to God and neighbor alike their due; *fortitude* provides the stamina to pursue the good, even amid difficulties; *temperance* offers perspective in evaluating sensual pleasures and counsels balance in our use of created things (1835-38). These human qualities are acquired by education, by deliberate and repeated acts, and are perfected by divine grace. For the Christian, the virtues are further developed by recourse to the sacraments and reliance on the Holy Spirit.

Next in line are the three theological virtues, so called because they pertain to our relationship with God, having "God for their origin, their motive, and their object—God known by faith, God hoped in and loved for his own sake" (1840). These three "inform all the moral virtues and give life to them" (1841). As St. Paul taught the Colossians, it is charity that binds all the virtues together in perfect harmony (3:14). In a most practical and helpful way, the catechism notes that one who possesses and is possessed by the virtues no longer relates to God in a fearful or servile manner; on the contrary, he is imbued with true spiritual freedom and knows the dignity of a child of God.

This discussion is rounded out by reference to the seven gifts of the Holy Spirit and the twelve fruits of the Holy Spirit. The former sustain us in living a moral life; the latter are the results of such a life and a foretaste of the life of heaven (1830-32).

Only now does conversation about sin make any sense. In other words, now that we know what God intended for us from the beginning—and still wants for his children—we can look ourselves squarely in the mirror and see how far off the mark we are (interestingly, the Greek word for sin, *hamartia*, actually means "missing the mark"). It is none other than Jesus, whose name means Savior, who can and wills to rescue us from our sins. Combining revelation and human experience, the catechism speaks of sin in two ways: "Sin is an utterance, a deed, or a desire contrary to the eternal law. It is an offense against God. It rises up against God in a disobedience contrary to the obedience of Christ." At a more experiential level, "sin is an act contrary to reason. It wounds man's nature and injures human solidarity" (1871-72).

As the First Epistle of John maintains, sins differ in gravity (1 Jn 16-17). The Church has enshrined that distinction into the categories of *mortal* sin, which "destroys charity in the heart of man by a grave violation of God's law," and *venial* sin, which "allows charity to subsist, even though it offends and wounds it" (1855). Relying on traditional norms for determining mortal sin and citing Pope John Paul II's *Reconciliatio et Paenitentia*, the text speaks of mortal sin as one "whose object is grave matter and which is also committed with full knowledge and deliberate consent" (1857). It likewise helps to specify "gravity" and gives principles for making such determinations personally.

We also read of excusing elements such as unintentional ignorance, external pressures, pathological disorders or passions that can "diminish the voluntary and free character of the offense" (1860). We are reminded that "mortal sin is a radical possibility of human freedom," which deprives one of sanctifying grace and, if unrepented before death, "causes exclusion from Christ's kingdom and the eternal death of hell" (1861). While acknowledging the lesser gravity of venial sins, the catechism nonetheless warns of the effects of such sins: weakening of charity; disposition toward mortal sin; and impeding progress in virtue. In the context of stressing the limitless nature of God's mercy, it tackles the question of the "[sin] *against the Holy Spirit*" by identifying it as that "hardness of heart [which] can lead to final impenitence and eternal loss" (1864).

In a very realistic vein, the catechism underscores how sin leads to yet more sin—personally and communally. In this way, we see how one's personal sins affect others and can eventually become the building blocks for "structures of sin" and "social sin" (1869).

The Human Community

Chapter Two is a reflection on the truism that no man is an island. Because every human being has the same ultimate calling, namely, union with God, we stand in solidarity with one another—or should do so. Utilizing the best of the Tradition of the Church, as well as the best insights from sociology, the catechism presents the Church's view of the human person in community. Two practical conclusions emerge. First, "society ought to promote the exercise of virtue, not obstruct it. It should be animated by a just hierarchy of values." Second, "where sin has perverted the social climate, it is necessary to call for the conversion of hearts and appeal to the grace of God." Establishing social reform firmly within the theological realm, the text declares that "there is no solution to the social question apart from the Gospel" (1895-96).

The section that follows deals with participation in social life and treats of concepts like authority, the common good, peace, security, personal responsibility, public life. It holds that "participation begins with education and culture" (1917). That is followed by an exposition on social justice, with terms like "respect," "equality," "dignity" and "solidarity" dotting the landscape (1929-39).

Law and Grace

Chapter Three considers God's salvation under the rubric of "law and grace" (1949). It speaks of the moral law in poetic language as "the work of divine Wisdom," "fatherly instruction" and "God's pedagogy" that "is at once firm in its precepts and, in its promises, worthy of love" (1950). Which is to say that it calls for the development of that mentality that prevailed among the ancient Hebrews who could sing of God's Law as a delight (cf. Ps 119), rather than a burden to be shunned. We are asked to recall that "all [human] law finds its first and ultimate truth in the eternal law [of God]" (1951). A marvelous discussion ensues on the meaning of the natural law, with a citation from the pagan Roman Cicero, highlighting how this law is indeed the common patrimony of the entire human race. Old Cicero declares, "For there is a true law: right reason. It is in conformity with nature, is diffused among all men, and is immutable and eternal; its orders summon to duty; its prohibitions turn away from offense . . . To replace it with a contrary law is a sacrilege; failure to apply even one of its provisions is forbidden; no one can abrogate it entirely" (1956). It was this very type of thinking that was posited in the founding of every major democracy in history; it is only this kind of analysis that can save them from self-destruction, either as whole societies or as the individuals that comprise them.

The catechism speaks of the nature and purpose of the Old Law and sees in it "a *preparation for the Gospel*" (1964). Some Jewish observers have taken offense at the suggestion that "their" Law is thus relegated to a "provisional" status. But the text need not be understood in a deprecatory manner; indeed, we read that the Old Law "provides a teaching which endures for ever, like the Word of God" (1963), all the while noting that it is perfected by the New Law (1984), which is seen as "the grace of the Holy Spirit received by faith in Christ, operating through charity. It finds expression above all in the Lord's Sermon on the Mount and uses the sacraments to communicate grace to us" (1983). Beyond that, the evangelical counsels of poverty, chastity and obedience are offered as "more direct ways" or "readier means" to observe the precepts of love of God and neighbor (1974).

Grace and Justification

This section of the catechism is not for the faint-hearted—and not surprisingly, for the entire Protestant Reformation revolved around the issues of grace and justification. According to St. Paul (particularly in his epistles to the Galatians and Romans), justification means being made "right" with God. That sounds simple enough, which is how most Fundamentalist preachers present the doctrine, but in reality, it is a very complex process. Following the New Testament and the Council of Trent most carefully, the catechism traces out the main lines of Catholic teaching on this topic. First, the Holy Spirit brings us to conversion, which in turn effects our justification, consisting of several components: it detaches us from sin; it causes us to accept God's righteousness (or justice) through faith in Christ; it was merited for us by the passion of the Lord; it establishes cooperation between God's grace and human freedom; and it entails the sanctification of the whole person (1990-95).

How does all of this spiritual activity occur? Through divine grace—which is God's *favor* or free, undeserved help—and "a *participation in the life of God*" (1996-97). It is important to stress that the grace of God is, above all else, divine in origin and that it accompanies us all along the road of justification and sanctification. In other words, God's grace is always a free gift of his and without that grace we cannot initiate any good work or bring it to completion. At the same time, it is essential to recall that grace cannot and will not be forced upon anyone; therefore, human cooperation is necessary. As St. Augustine put it, "God created us without us; but He did not will to save us without us." Therefore, the union of the divine and human, which began in the Incarnation, continues to be the pattern for salvation.

Traditionally, Catholic theology has distinguished several classes of grace: sanctifying (that which perfects the soul, enabling it to live with God and in His love); actual (the assistance to respond to particular situations according to God's will); sacramental (gifts proper to the different sacraments). Yet another form of grace is what the New Testament calls a "*charism*," that is, a gift (ordinary or extraordinary) that is "oriented toward sanctifying grace and [is] intended for the common good of the Church" (2003).

On the thorny Reformation question of merit (and one still quite neuralgic in Evangelical and especially Fundamentalist circles), the catechism holds that "we can have merit in God's sight only because of God's free plan to associate man with the work of his grace. Merit is to be ascribed in the first place to the grace of God, and secondly to man's collaboration. Man's merit is due to God" (2025). For some Catholics who think they can "earn" salvation (in some kind of crass *quid pro quo* arrangement), this may come as news. Furthermore, "no one can merit the initial grace which is at the origin of conversion." That having been said, the text goes on to strike the balance between the human and divine once more: "Moved by the Holy Spirit, we can merit for ourselves and for others all the graces needed to attain eternal life, as well as necessary temporal goods" (2027).

And finally, what is the goal of all this? Christian holiness, which is but another name for "intimate union with Christ" (2014). This does not just happen, however, for as the Lord Jesus himself taught, it requires the taking up of one's cross daily, in imitation of him: "The way of perfection passes by way of the Cross" (2015). Believers look toward their everlasting union with God in hope and pray for the grace of final perseverance.

Between now and the hour of our death, God calls us to lead a moral life—a godly life that will prepare us to live with him for all eternity, a life which is anticipated through the Church that Christ founded. In that Church, we hear the summons to holiness; we are strengthened with the sacraments which give us the grace to do God's holy will; we receive the message of truth and the challenge of the Gospel; we are given the commandments of God and of the Church, which is his spokesman—Christ's Bride and our Mother. Our response to this needs to be intense gratitude. Or as the catechism puts it, "Thus a true *filial spirit toward the Church* can develop among Christians. It is the normal flowering of the baptismal grace which has begotten us in the womb of the Church and made us members of the Body of Christ. In her motherly care, the Church grants us the mercy of God which prevails over all our sins and is especially at work in the sacrament of reconciliation.

With a mother's foresight, she also lavishes on us day after day in her liturgy the nourishment of the Word and Eucharist of the Lord" (2040). It is in this way that we are able to obey the Ten Commandments, to which we now turn our attention.

SECTION TWO: THE TEN COMMANDMENTS
Love and the Commandments

The catechism's treatment of the Ten Commandments begins, like *Veritatis Splendor*, with the parable of the rich young man who desires perfection and has kept all the commandments from his youth. The point, of course, is that observing the commandments is but the first (even if necessary) step on the road to holiness, which is achieved by loving God and neighbor totally. Those who adopt an antinomian posture are brought to understand that "by his life and by his preaching Jesus attested to the permanent validity of the Decalogue" (2076), that body of laws which lies at the very heart of the covenant between God and the Chosen People. Those who consider the Ten Commandments to be "too negative" are led to an appreciation of how they offer a genuine "way of life" that leads to holiness by bringing people to discover God's holy will for them; hence, their inclusion in the Ark of the Covenant.

An excellent point is also made of the fact that these "ten words" are addressed by God to believers in the singular—not the plural—to underscore the very personal nature of the covenant relationship (although the covenant is obviously and equally a communal affair) (2063). The Decalogue, we read, imposes *"grave obligations"* (2072), but one is likewise promised divine assistance in the process of integrating these laws into one's personal life: "What God commands he makes possible by his grace" (2082).

THE FIRST THREE COMMANDMENTS
The First Commandment: "I am the Lord your God . . ."

The first three commandments combine to spell out how to love God with "all your heart, with all your soul, and with all your mind." "The first commandment summons man to believe in God, to hope in him, and to love him above all else" (2134). Faith is the virtue that undergirds this commandment, demanding that we reject whatever is opposed to faith. Thus, obstinate doubting or even unbelief, heresy (denial of one or more doctrines of the Catholic Faith), apostasy (total rejection of the Christian Faith) and schism (refusal to submit to the Sovereign Pontiff) are all sins against the theological virtue of faith.

Sins against hope are despair by which "man ceases to hope" in God as his personal salvation and "presumption" that may be of two kinds: man trusting in his own powers to save himself or one's expectation of obtaining "forgiveness without conversion and glory without merit" (2092). Charity is violated by indifference, ingratitude, lukewarmness, spiritual laziness and hatred for God.

In effect, the First Commandment protects the virtue of religion, the first act of which must always be adoration. In this regard, we see Mary as the most perfect adorer as she recognizes her own nothingness and God's graciousness to her at one and the same time, praising him for being who he is and for doing what he has done in her life (Lk 1:46-49). Following adoration come prayer, sacrifice and promises or vows, which seek to give flesh and bones to the obligation to adore God.

An extensive discussion ensues on ways in which human beings worship false gods today: superstition, idolatry (included here are both polytheism and satanism but also the worship of "power, pleasure, race, ancestors, the state, money, etc." (2113)), divination (including astrology and recourse to mediums), and magic. Also condemned by the First Commandment are sins of irreligion: testing God in words or deeds, sacrilege (especially against the Blessed Sacrament), and simony. The phenomena of atheism and agnosticism are well presented, too.

On the matter of "graven images," the catechism notes that they are not forbidden by the First Commandment since no worship is given to them but is directed beyond the images to the reality being signified, as is taught by Nicea II and Aquinas alike. A worthwhile observation is also made: That even the Old Testament itself did not have an absolute prohibition against such things, for we find God commanding the fashioning of the bronze serpent and the Ark of the Covenant with the cherubim (2130). Finally, the topic is referred to the mystery of the Incarnation, whereby God did indeed take on a human form, so that attempts to image him are not blasphemous (2141).

The Second Commandment: "The name of the Lord is Holy."

Moving on to the Second Commandment, we are made aware of the need to respect the holiness of God's Name, which we must always "bless, praise and glorify." Sins against this injunction consist of breaking "*promises* made to others in God's name [which] engage the divine honor, fidelity, truthfulness, and authority" (2147). Also forbidden is blasphemy, which "use[s] . . . the name of God, of Jesus Christ, of the Virgin Mary and of the saints in an offensive way" (2162), as well as either casual or magical uses of the divine name. The Second Commandment also takes within its purview false oaths or perjury.

An excellent passage on the sacredness of human names is likewise offered. Interestingly, perhaps in an effort to go beyond both the Rite of Baptism and the Code of Canon Law, it calls for the giving of a distinctly Christian name at Baptism

(2165); the former documents merely indicate that a name conferred cannot be *contrary* to Christian virtue. A fine meditation on the sign of the cross is given and the wonderful reminder that "God calls each one by name" (2167), again highlighting the individual's relation with Almighty God.

The Third Commandment: "Remember the Sabbath Day, to keep it holy."

The Third Commandment enjoins one to keep holy the Sabbath. The Hebrews of old observed this law for three reasons:
to remember God's creative activity and rest; to commemorate
their liberation from slavery in Egypt; as a sign of the unbreak-
able covenant between God and the Chosen People. Christians
accept all that, change the day to the first of the week and
celebrate God's re-creation of humanity in and through the
Resurrection of Christ. For this reason, Christians are required
to worship the Lord through the offering of the Eucharistic Sacrifice each Sunday, which is "the foremost holy day of obligation" (2177); also mentioned are the other holy days of obligation. "Those who deliberately fail in this obligation commit a
grave sin," we are instructed (2181). As part of the rationale
given for worshipping with the entire assembly of believers,
the assertion of St. John Chrysostom is cited: "You cannot pray
at home as at church, where there is a great multitude, where
exclamations are cried out to God as from one great heart, and
where there is something more: the union of minds, the ac-
cord of souls, the bond of charity, the prayers of the priests"
(2179).

Last of all, we come upon the Sabbath rest, which calls for
"the faithful . . . to refrain from engaging in work or activities
that hinder the worship owed to God, the joy proper to the
Lord's Day, the performance of the works of mercy, and the

appropriate relaxation of mind and body" (2185). A special plea is sent up to use the Lord's Day "to cultivate their familial, cultural, social, and religious lives" and not to engage in activities that will force others to forego the joy of the Sabbath by making them work (2194-95). While Catholics in the United States are generally better at Mass attendance than most others in the world, our observance of the Sabbath rest may well be the worst and, therefore, in need of the correction given in the catechism.

Having learned our duties toward God, we are now prepared to hear of what we owe our neighbor.

COMMANDMENTS FOUR AND FIVE
The Fourth Commandment: "Honor your father and your mother . . ."

Having considered man's obligations to God on the first table of the Decalogue, we now move to the second for our responsibilities toward our neighbor. We begin with the duty to honor one's parents, which the catechism observes indicates "the order of charity," that is, one starts to love the neighbor closest to home and then in ever-widening circles from there, including not only one's parents but also all legitimately "vested with [God's] authority"(2197): rendering "honor, affection, and gratitude" to one's elders and ancestors," teachers and government officials (2199). Thus, it contains within itself all the following commandments regarding respect for the life and property of others and so serves as "one of the foundations of the social doctrine of the Church" (2198). It is significant that this is the only commandment that also holds out a promise for its observance: "Honor your father and your mother, that your days may be long in the land which the Lord your God gives you" (2200). Conversely, disregard for this law of God brings in its wake grave disasters for entire communities and for individual persons.

The catechism defines a family in this way: "A man and a woman united in marriage, together with their children, form a family" (2202). This is obviously quite different from various descriptions we find in the civil realm today. Because of the family's origin in God (and not as any kind of human construct), it has rights that precede "any recognition by public authority"; put bluntly, the family imposes on the State, and not the other way around (2202). Within the family, we encounter a gathering of "persons equal in dignity," with "manifold responsibilities, rights and duties" (2203). With Vatican II, the catechism prefers to reflect theologically on the family as "a *domestic Church*"—"a community of faith, hope, and charity" of "singular importance," an "image of the communion of the Father and the Son in the Holy Spirit." Herein one also finds its procreative and educative functions, mirroring "the Father's work of creation." Likewise, it is "called to partake of the prayer and sacrifice of Christ" and must exhibit an "evangelizing and missionary" dimension as well (2204-05).

Sociologically speaking, "the family is the *original cell of social life*" since it is there that "one can learn moral values, begin to honor God, and make good use of freedom. Family life is an initiation into life in society." This is also the place where people should learn concern and responsibility for "the old, the sick, the handicapped, and the poor." When families need help themselves, they should be able to count on it from various organs of society, but the catechism cautions against violation of "the principle of subsidiarity," whereby "larger communities should take care not to usurp the family's prerogatives or interfere in its life" (2207-09).

Relying on John Paul II's *Familiaris Consortio*, deemed by

many to be a genuine *Magna Carta* of family rights, the catechism delineates those rights, which include the right to: "establish a family, have children, and bring them up in keeping with the family's own moral and religious convictions"; "profess [and transmit] one's faith"; and "form associations with other families and so to have representation before civil authority." Also highlighted are rights to civil protection of marital and family stability, medical treatment, security from the dangers of drugs, pornography and alcohol (2211).

And so, one can see how this commandment "*illuminates other relations in society,*" both ecclesiastical and civil. It makes a special point of stressing the familial nature of life in the Church since all the baptized are "children of our mother, the Church" (2212).

Family Relationships

With St. Paul, the text teaches that "divine fatherhood is the source of human fatherhood." With this connection in mind, it is easier to understand why filial piety is so highly esteemed a virtue. We read that "as long as a child lives at home with his parents, the child should obey in all that they ask of him when it is for his good or that of the family"; similarly, that kind of obedience is to be transferred to one's teachers who stand *in loco parentis*. Needless to say, one must never obey what is clearly an immoral or unjust order. As children grow up, their relationship to their parents changes, so that the requirement to obey ceases upon their emancipation, but that of respect never does. Furthermore, as the parents age, filial responsibility may well call for increased activity on behalf of the parents. Concern for family harmony also dictates that relations among brothers and sisters be governed by charity. A particular plea is made for extending gratitude toward those who introduced one to life in the Church and have nurtured it: parents, other family members, priests, teachers, friends (2214-20).

With reciprocity, the catechism turns its attention to parental obligations, starting with the wholesome counsel that "the fecundity of conjugal love cannot be reduced solely to the procreation of children, but must extend to their moral education and their spiritual formation," going on to hold that the *"role of parents* [in this task] is of such importance that it is almost impossible to provide an adequate substitute." Children are not chattel; "Parents must regard their children as *children of God* and respect them as *human persons."* Parents are required to make a home for their children and educate them in virtuous living; they must also see themselves as the first evangelizers of them, initiating them into life in the Church "at an early age," teaching them to pray, offering them the "witness of a Christian life," and providing them with a basic catechesis that "precedes, accompanies, and enriches other forms of instruction in the faith."

Continuing to view family life in terms of mutuality, the text observes that children can "in [their] turn contribute to the *growth in holiness* of their parents." Parents are reminded of their responsibility to choose schools for their children that inculcate and foster Christian values. At the same time, the State is exhorted to provide the appropriate means for parents of all economic backgrounds to be able to exercise their God-given right to freedom of choice in education. A final note concerns the obligation of parents to grasp that, "family ties are important but not absolute." Hence, parents must realize that their task requires them to teach their young, first of all, "to *follow Jesus."* Certainly taking the measure of parental resistance to priestly and religious vocations so often exhibited today, the catechism enjoins parents to accept and respect such calls and decisions "with joy and thanksgiving" (2221-33).

Civil Authority

A final section deals with civil authority that can never "command or establish what is contrary to the dignity of persons and the natural law." When authority is just and functions properly, Christians should see in such superiors "[the] representatives of God"; a good and holy patriotism enables citizens to recognize their civic duties by loving and serving their country. That concern for the common good will be evidenced in the willingness to pay taxes, to vote, and to defend one's country. A particular appeal is made for better-off nations to be charitable and open to immigrants who come seeking a better way of life or even asylum. For their part, immigrants must respect the "material and spiritual heritage" of their host country, obey its laws and contribute to its well-being.

When human laws impinge on divine laws, believers must disobey, following the Lord's counsel to render to God before Caesar and the insight of the apostolic Church that it is necessary to "obey God rather than men." When public authority becomes tyrannical, Christians may rightly rebel, but resorting to armed conflict is to be avoided strenuously and its moral exercise is hemmed in by a multitude of restrictions. Finally, we are led to appreciate the role of the Church vis-a-vis the political community: Her role is supra-national and supra-political, that she may always be "the sign and the safeguard of the transcendent character of the human person." This does not mean that the Church has no political function; on the contrary, she is to be the bearer of a moral judgment, especially "whenever the fundamental rights of man or the salvation of souls requires it" (2234-46). And thus, we can comprehend how respect for parents and love for the family does indeed affect every segment of society, bringing the blessing promised by Almighty God to the Hebrews of old.

The Fifth Commandment: "You shall not kill."

"You shall not kill" (2258), enjoins the Lord God. This section of the catechism spells out the implications of that short injunction. The rationale for it is found in *Donum Vitae* of the Congregation for the Doctrine of the Faith, which speaks of the sacredness of human life in these terms: "God alone is the Lord of life from its beginning until its end: no one can under any circumstance claim for himself the right directly to destroy an innocent human being" (2258). The complete essay on this commandment is suffused with this notion of respect for human life, created in the image and likeness of God, providing us with an absolute norm that is "universally valid: it obliges each and everyone, always and everywhere" (2261). The commandment found in the Hebrew Scriptures is fleshed out yet more in Christ's Sermon on the Mount, where He counsels would-be disciples to turn the other cheek and to love their enemies.

But is the prohibition against killing truly an absolute? What about exceptions for legitimate self-defense? This is not an exception, notes the catechism, citing Aquinas in this connection: "The act of self-defense can have a double effect: the preservation of one's own life; and the killing of the aggressor . . . The one is intended, the other is not" (2263)—a subtle and important distinction. The text goes on to argue that self-defense "can be not only a right but a grave duty" for one responsible for the welfare of others or for the common good (2265). While holding to the traditional statement of the right of the State to exact capital punishment, it also advises recourse to non-violent solutions and cautions against vengeance.

Attacks on Human Life

In discussing direct and willful homicide, the catechism singles out "infanticide, fratricide, parricide" as especially worthy of condemnation (2268), as well as eugenics programs— even and maybe even particularly when mandated by public authority. Not surprisingly, an extensive presentation is made on abortion, wherein we read that human life must be protected and guaranteed all rights "from the first moment of his existence," that is, "from the moment of conception" (2270). Careful to situate this teaching within history, it comments that this has been the Catholic position "since the first century" as found in the *Didache* and that "this teaching has not changed" (2271). It goes on to explain the canonical penalty of excommunication leveled for this crime against God and man and observes that this offense is so heinous because "the inalienable right to life of every innocent human individual is a *constitutive element of a civil society and its legislation*" (2273). While acknowledging the liceity of prenatal diagnostic testing, it likewise warns that such diagnosis must be used to foster human life and never employed in such manner that it amounts to "a death sentence" (2274).

Moving to the other end of the life continuum, the catechism deals with euthanasia, condemning it with equal intensity as "morally unacceptable. Thus an act or omission which, of itself or by intention, causes death in order to eliminate suffering constitutes a murder gravely contrary to the dignity of the human person and to the respect due to the living God, his Creator. The error of judgment into which one can fall in good faith does not change the nature of this murderous act, which must always be forbidden and excluded" (2277). The usual distinction is made between ordinary and extraordinary means and on the need for the patient to be involved in such decisions, but special attention is given to the need to provide normal care which is the sufferer's right as well as "a special form of disinterested charity" (2279).

Suicide is treated as an act against "the sovereign Master," since thereby human beings arrogate to themselves decisions about human existence. It is also seen as "contrary to the just love of self. It likewise offends love of neighbor because it unjustly breaks the ties of solidarity" within the various societies of man; finally it "is contrary to love for the living God." Cooperation in this activity "is contrary to the moral law." With sensitivity, the authors remind that "grave psychological disturbances, anguish, or grave fear of hardship, suffering, or torture can diminish the responsibility of the one committing suicide." Therefore, one "should not despair of the eternal salvation" of such persons; the text even postulates the possibility that God gives people in these straits "the opportunity for salutary repentance" (2280-83).

Human Dignity

The next major division is entitled "Respect for the Dignity of Persons" (2284). Included for consideration is the sin of scandal and the need to care for one's health. This latter topic must never devolve into "the *cult of the body*" but should lead to the cultivation of the virtue of temperance "to *avoid every kind of excess*," which can be abuses of food, alcohol, tobacco and medicine (2289-90). Drunken driving and speeding are cited as culpable actions. Scientific research is praised when conducted with the good of the person in view and within proper parameters. A similar evaluation is made of organ transplants, with the added admonition that "it is morally inadmissible directly to bring about the disabling mutilation or death of a human being, even in order to delay the death of other persons" (2296).

Classified together as "morally wrong" are kidnapping, hostage-taking, terrorism, and torture, as well as amputations, mutilations or sterilizations which are not "for strictly therapeutic medical reasons" (2297). Respect for the dying is highlighted, especially by permitting them to die "in dignity and peace" and providing them with access to the sacraments. Burying the dead is, of course, a corporal work of mercy. Autopsies are permissible when performed for legal or scientific motives. "The free gift of organs after death is legitimate and can be meritorious." Finally, it is recalled that "the Church permits cremation, provided that it does not demonstrate a denial of faith in the resurrection of the body" (2299-2301).

Fostering Peace

Safeguarding peace is the concern of the last section (2302-17). With *Gaudium et Spes*, the catechism notes that "peace is not merely the absence of war"; with St. Augustine, it teaches that peace is "the tranquillity of order." "Earthly peace," we read, "is the image and fruit of the *peace of Christ*, '[the] Prince of peace,'" who achieved this peace by the blood of his cross, thus reconciling God and man and making of his Church, "the sacrament of the unity of the human race and of its union with God." He who is, as St. Paul taught, "our peace" likewise declares, "Blessed are the peacemakers." Hence, at a personal level, that anger which is "to desire vengeance" and deliberate hatred are obstacles to peace; such attitudes then lead to communal manifestations, endangering peace on a grander scale.

The catechism teaches that "all citizens and all governments are obliged to work for the avoidance of war." That said, it goes on to speak of "the right of lawful self-defense" and reasserts the "just war" doctrine, outlining the conditions necessary for its deployment. Similarly, it declares that public authorities have the right to "impose on citizens the *obligations necessary for national defense.*" At the same time, for reasons of conscience, people can refuse to bear arms, but still have a duty "to serve the human community in some other way." In classical style, we are reminded of the necessity that "non-combatants, wounded soldiers, and prisoners must be respected and treated humanely." Although certainly expecting cooperation with military superiors, the catechism condemns "[a] blind obedience" that would be complicitous in crimes against moral norms for waging war. The arms build-up is denounced, and a strong cautionary word is sounded for this approach to be used as a deterrent to war.

For those who operate from political categories without reference to the perennial truths of natural law and Catholic theology, there should be at least one thing to irk or prick the conscience of just about everyone so disposed. For the sons and daughters of the Church, who understand and accept the meaning of the sacredness of human life, everything found here will reflect a marvelous consistency and a happy reconciliation of conflicting claims.

THE SIXTH AND NINTH COMMANDMENTS

In examining the sixth and ninth commandments, we follow the lead of Christ himself, who took cognizance of the sixth law of the Decalogue and immediately connected it to that desire or lust which makes adultery possible and even probable (cf. Mt 5:27-8). The underlying psychology and theology of this portion of the catechism is found in the assertion that "love is the fundamental and innate vocation of every human being" (2392).

Not by accident, this line is a quote from Pope John Paul II whose thought dots the landscape of this entire treatise. What emerges is a holistic and personalist view of sexuality that "affects all aspects of the human person in the unity of his body and soul." Sexual identity is likewise seen as requiring an appreciation of the difference and the complementarity of the sexes, both of which are equal, both made in the image and likeness of God, and both called in marriage to "[imitate] in the flesh the Creator's generosity and fecundity." In line with the constant Tradition of the Church, the sixth commandment concerns not only the question of adultery but the whole of human sexuality (2331-36).

The Sixth Commandment: "You shall not commit adultery."
The Ninth Commandment: "You shall not desire your neighbor's wife."

This discussion is situated within the overall context of "The Vocation to Chastity" that is proper to every human being. It is also focused on the development of that "integrity" of life that occurs when one learns self-mastery and does not merely respond to norms imposed by some authority external to the person (2337-38). The advice offered is at once sound theology and excellent practical pastoral counsel; the pursuit of virtue is stressed far more than the avoidance of vice. We are wisely reminded that chastity is not something achieved once for all, but involves consistent effort and constant recourse to the grace of God throughout one's entire life.

Chastity should not be perceived as a negative but as the expression of friendship at its deepest level. St. Ambrose saw this clearly when he wrote that chastity existed in various forms, corresponding to the several states in life. The catechism makes mention of the chastity important for the engaged, so that their pre-marital continence demonstrates "[their] mutual respect" and also serves as "an apprenticeship in fidelity, and the hope of receiving one another from God." Prudently, it cautions them to "reserve for marriage the expressions of affection that belong to married love" (2350). Lust, masturbation, fornication, pornography, prostitution and rape are all denounced as offenses against chastity (2351-56), with convincing rationale given for these positions.

A very forthright, nuanced and helpful presentation on homosexuality is made. "Its psychological genesis remains largely unexplained"; nevertheless, the moral conclusion is inescapable: "Homosexual acts are intrinsically disordered" because "they close the sexual act to the gift of life" and hence "under no circumstances can they be approved." The text continues: "The number of men and women who have deep-seated homosexual tendencies is not negligible. They do not choose their homosexual condition"; it is, for them "a trial. They must be accepted with respect, compassion, and sensitivity. Every sign of unjust discrimination in their regard should be avoided." Such people, "if they are Christians, [are called] to unite to the sacrifice of the Lord's Cross the difficulties they may encounter from their condition." They are called to a life of chastity and, taking advantage of all the aids of the interior life, "gradually and resolutely" should see themselves attain to "Christian perfection" (2357-59). Once again, the Church's moderation stands out against extremes that condemn or condone.

Marital Love and Openness to Life

Turning its attention to "The Love of Husband and Wife" (2360), the catechism notes that this is not something "simply biological, but concerns the innermost being of the human person as such" since it signifies the reciprocal gift by which spouses enrich each other "in joy and gratitude" (2361-62). The source of such joy and pleasure is sexuality, which has "the twofold end" within holy matrimony: "the good of the spouses themselves and the transmission of life." Soberly, the text stresses that "these two meanings or values of marriage cannot be separated without altering the couple's spiritual life and compromising the goods of marriage and the future of the family." This demands "fidelity and fecundity" (2363).

By living marital fidelity, the Christian couple "bear witness to this mystery [of Christ and his Church] before the world" (2365). In regard to fruitfulness, the catechism declares that "a child does not come from without as something added on to the mutual love of the spouses, but springs from the very heart of that mutual giving," which is why Pope Paul VI was so right to teach in *Humanae Vitae* that "each and every marriage act must remain open to the transmission of life," for no such act of man should ever contradict the express will of God who desires that it always signify the unitive and procreative at one and the same time (2366).

With this in mind, only "for just reasons" can couples decide "to space the births of their children," always ensuring that such a decision does not arise from "selfishness but is in conformity with the generosity appropriate to responsible parenthood. . . . These methods [relying on periodic continence] respect the bodies of the spouses, encourage tenderness between them, and favor the education of an authentic freedom" (2368-70). Needless to say, any forcible action on the part of the State that intrudes into the sanctuary of marriage is to be deemed reprehensible.

Reflecting on the concept of large families, the catechism observes that both Scripture and the Church's perennial thrust regard them as "a sign of God's blessing and the parents' generosity" (2373). Moving on to couples incapable of child-bearing, the text speaks with compassion but also, echoing *Donum*

Vitae, concludes that techniques like artificial insemination are "gravely immoral" and cheat a child out of birth from an act of love (2376). Artificial conception fails the moral test for the same reason as artificial contraception: both dissociate the unitive and procreative elements of the marital act, albeit for opposite goals. Even given the noble desire to conceive, one must recall that "a child is not something *owed* to one, but is a *gift*" (2378). It goes on to emphasize that "physical sterility is not an absolute evil" and that it can actually become a source of spiritual fruitfulness, especially when couples demonstrate "their generosity by adopting abandoned children or performing demanding services for others" (2379).

Not surprisingly, we find that "adultery, divorce, polygamy, and free union are grave offenses against the dignity of marriage" (2400). Considerable space is given over to an explanation of the Church's teaching on divorce, along with particular attention given to its implications for children and society. Taking on *"trial marriage,"* the text asserts that "human love does not tolerate 'trial marriages.' It demands a total and definitive gift of persons to one another" (2391).

Inducements to Unchastity

To this point, we have been considering direct violations of chastity, but we must also give due attention to things which lead to such violations. Thus, when Our Lord spoke with such vehemence against lust, he was well within the whole Jewish tradition of building a wall around the Torah, that is, forbidding what could be seen as a less grievous offense, so as to guard against the commission of a more serious one. It is in this light that we need to look at the proscriptions of the ninth commandment, which seeks to help humans control concupiscence, that drive which Christian theology has identified in a particular way with carnal desire.

What is needed here is nothing less than "[the] purification of the heart," declared "blessed" by Christ in the Sermon on the Mount. "The struggle against carnal lust [and human experience certainly confirms it is a battle] involves purifying the heart and practicing temperance," so that people begin to view all things according to the mind and heart of God Himself; similarly, it "demands prayer, the practice of chastity, purity of intention and of vision" (2530-32). These are not puritanical suggestions but are grounded in common sense and the tried and true methods of growth in virtue, as well as a salutary respect for the dignity of persons. The text encourages modesty in dress, discretion, education in decency for children and adolescents, and the purification of the social climate. Those uncomfortable with such a program for fostering decency reveal "an erroneous conception of human freedom" (2526), for whatever leads people to moral degradation is the most enslaving of all.

THE SEVENTH AND TENTH COMMANDMENTS
The Seventh Commandment: "You shall not steal."

"The seventh commandment enjoins the practice of justice and charity in the administration of earthly goods and the fruits of men's labor" (2451), reads the catechism's summary related to this law of God. Operative language throughout are expressions like: the common good, human dignity, fundamental needs, human solidarity—in short, terminology from the Church's social encyclicals, but especially the thought of Pope John Paul II. While clearly and strongly supporting the right to private property, the text reminds us that that right is not absolute, for the earth was originally given to "the whole human race" (2402). Hence, "the *universal destination of goods* remains primordial" (2403); this requires of public authority the regulation of "the legitimate exercise of the right to ownership" (2406).

Temperance

As we look at how people should approach temporal goods, Christians will be guided by "the practice of the virtue of *temperance,* so as to moderate attachment to this world's goods," as well as justice and solidarity (2407). Theft is a clear violation of the seventh commandment and of justice; it is defined as "usurping another's property against the reasonable will of the owner." However, it is not a question of theft if the consent of the owner is presumed or "if refusal is contrary to reason and the universal destination of goods" (2408). In other words, basic human needs (like food, shelter and clothing) supersede one's right to private property. Other sins against justice include deliberate retention of lost or stolen goods; fraud in commerce; giving unjust wages; and price-fixing. Similarly, one is obliged to honor promises and contracts and to pay one's debts. When injustice has been done, reparation must be made.

"*Games of chance* or *wagers* are not in themselves contrary to justice. They become morally unacceptable when they deprive someone of what is necessary to provide for his needs and those of others" (2413). Again, one can see Catholic moderation here—no unnecessary blanket condemnations but a call to use right judgment or prudence, with a proper sense of priorities. Slavery is proscribed because treating people like merchandise is a denial of their personal dignity.

Also obligatory is what *political correctness* today might label an *ecological sense.* Although the catechism notes that man was given dominion over all creation, it also reminds us that this is not absolute: "It is limited by concern for the quality of life of his neighbor, including generations to come; it requires a religious respect for the integrity of creation" (2415). A tender love for animals is counselled, relying on the example of saints like Francis of Assisi or Philip Neri; but this is not lopsided, for it also acknowledges the right to use animals for food and clothing, as well as for medical experimentation to benefit man—albeit not to cause them useless suffering. At the same time, the catechism chastises those who spend inordinate amounts of money on animals, resources that could be better used to alleviate human misery.

Justice among Individuals and Nations

In treating the social doctrine of the Church, the text holds that any system completely determined by economic considerations "is contrary to human dignity" and is thus unacceptable; for such reasons, the Church, it says, rejected theories like communism and socialism, but has also uttered strong cautions in regard to capitalism, always keeping in view "a just hierarchy of values and . . . the common good" (2424-25). Human work, à la John Paul II, is seen as proceeding from the dignity of one created in the image and likeness of the Creator-God; it also unites one with Christ's own redemptive work. Reminiscent of Blessed José-Maria Escrivà, the text teaches that "work can be a means of sanctification and a way of animating earthly realities with the Spirit of Christ" (2427). Through it all, however, one must never forget that "work is for man, not man for work" (2428). The responsibility of the State in this sphere is to provide the needed guarantees, "so that those who work and produce can enjoy the fruits of their labors and thus feel encouraged to work efficiently and honestly" and to watch over and conduct "the exercise of human rights in the economic sector" (2431). Rights delineated include access to work, a just wage and striking (when necessary).

In turning to justice among nations, the catechism again falls back on the rubric of "solidarity," as rich nations are instructed regarding their "grave moral responsibility" toward poorer ones (2439). Direct aid, reform of institutions, and overall development of human society are all discussed as ways of meeting this obligation. Such social action is, according to the catechism and Vatican II and the present Pontiff, preeminently the work of the laity, who are especially suited and deputed "to animate temporal realities with Christian commitment, by which they show that they are witnesses and agents of peace and justice" (2442).

Reflection on the seventh commandment ends with a meditation on the Christian meaning of love for the poor, which love—we are told—"is incompatible with immoderate love of riches or their selfish use" (2445). Some powerful citations from Fathers of the Church like John Chrysostom and Gregory the Great should help all realize that the Church's love for the poor has indeed been part of "her constant tradition," neither a novelty of the twentieth century nor a dispensable commodity for those seeking a comfortable religion that never hits one's wallet or pocketbook (2444).

The Tenth Commandment: "You shall not desire your neighbor's goods."

Such a teaching is likewise a fitting point of departure for an examination of the tenth commandment that "forbids avarice arising from a passion for riches and their attendant power" (2552). Very wisely, the text connects such drives to incipient forms of idolatry. In addition to avarice, this commandment likewise prohibits envy (a capital sin), which is described as "sadness at the sight of another's goods and the immoderate desire to have them for oneself." It is called a "capital" sin be-cause envy, like its six brothers, can easily lead to other sins (e.g., theft, hatred, even murder) (2553).

The catechism astutely moves on immediately to provide a remedy, which is to be found in the development of Christian virtue that fosters the desires of the Spirit, like benevolence, humility and abandonment to the providence of God (2555). It also means seeking to become "poor in spirit," which is the precondition for entering into the Kingdom of heaven, but that final goal cannot occur when one is weighed down by ex-cessive desires of a materialistic nature (2556). The one de-sire that keeps one from sin and guarantees access to the Kingdom is summed up in the line, "I want to see God." That desire is good and holy, and there is no commandment against it (2557).

THE EIGHTH COMMANDMENT
The Eighth Commandment: "You shall not bear false witness . . ."

The eighth commandment is concerned with the necessity of telling the truth. This topic is dealt with in a most interest-ing fashion in the catechism, from the perspective of the obli-gation of the People of God to be witnesses of God before the world. Therefore, all our words and actions must be clear, un-equivocal signs of the truth of God; failures in that regard "un-dermine the foundations of the covenant" (2464). The central-ity of truth in the revelation of God to man is stressed. Indeed, even a cursory review of a biblical concordance turns up more than 350 entries for "truth" or related words (2465). And so, with this in mind, it should come as no surprise that Christ, the Word of God from all eternity, chose to identify himself precisely as *the Truth* (2466).

PART THREE: LIFE IN CHRIST

Witnessing to the Truth and Failures to Do So

The importance of truth-telling is highlighted by some strong citations from Aquinas who grounds this obligation in the confidence human beings need to have in each other if they are going to live together. The text also locates this need in the dignity of the human person as *image of God*, the source of all truth. When asked to witness to the truth, especially regarding one's faith, the Christian will follow the example of Christ before Pilate as he proclaimed his mission on earth to be nothing less than "bear[ing] witness to the truth" (2471). In this connection, an excellent discussion of martyrdom (which comes from the Greek word for "witness") is given. Thus, we see that even as highly as a believer cherishes human life, testimony to eternal truth is a yet higher value. In referring to the acts of the martyrs, the catechism—in poetic and profound manner—speaks of these documents as "form[ing] the archives of truth written in letters of blood" (2474).

With the positive encouragement to live according to the truth now in place, we can consider offenses against the truth. Rash judgment (accepting as true without sufficient foundation the moral defect of one's neighbor), slander (revealing the hidden faults of others to those who have no right to the information) and calumny (communicating untruths about another) are all sins against the eighth commandment; "detraction and calumny destroy the *reputation and honor of one's neighbor*" (2479). This right to a good name is a fundamental right of every human being, and unjust attacks on it must be repaired through retraction and any other means that can help undo the damage of the original act, which reparation should be "moral and sometimes material" (2487). Flattery and boasting are also mentioned as inappropriate activities that compromise the truth and endanger human relationships.

Outright lying receives comprehensive treatment. Its definition is given by St. Augustine as consisting in the "speaking a falsehood with the intention of deceiving" (2482). The text goes on to note that this means "lead[ing] into error someone who has the right to know the truth" (2483). What about lying to save someone's life or to protect another's reputation? "The good and safety of others, respect for privacy, and the the common good are sufficient reasons for being silent about what ought not be known or for making use of a discreet language. The duty to avoid scandal often commands strict discretion. No one is bound to reveal the truth to someone who does not have the right to know it" (2489). The most "sacred" and "inviolable" of secrets is, of course, what is revealed in the Sacrament of Penance; that "the *secret of the sacrament of reconciliation*" is so absolute that a confessor who would violate that trust is automatically excommunicated (2490). But other professionals have similar obligations, albeit in less stringent form: military personnel, physicians, lawyers. Taking cognizance of the media's effort to pry into the private lives of public persons unnecessarily, the text condemns this as an unwarranted assault on their privacy and liberty.

Truth in the Media

The next section is concerned with "The Use of the Social Communications Media," which must always be viewed as being "at the service of the common good." Furthermore, this undergirds the conviction that "society has a right to information based on truth, freedom, justice, and solidarity" (2493-94). All of this must stem from a deep "knowledge and respect for others" (2495), so that a genuine "freedom of information" can occur without, however, falling into defamation or attempts to "[manipulate] public opinion" (2498). The noble vocation of journalism—whether print or electronic—is clearly delineated; how much that is accepted and/or lived by contemporary practitioners of the art should be the subject of much soul-searching and debate within the profession.

Finally, we are brought to a reflection on "Truth, Beauty, and Sacred Art." Truth, we read, "is beauty in itself" (2500). This beauty was first revealed by Almighty God not in words but in the act of creation, whereby he began to convey the truth about himself and our world. Quite logically, then, man (his image) "also expresses the truth of his relationship with God the Creator by the beauty of his artistic works," a class of endeavor unique to man as it arises from his commitment to "truth and love of beings," in imitation of the God of creation (2501).

Sacred art is an even more elevated form of the communication of the truth when it performs its proper function, namely, "evoking and glorifying, in faith and adoration, the transcendent mystery of God—the surpassing invisible beauty of truth and love visible in Christ . . . spiritual beauty of God is reflected in the most holy Virgin Mother of God, the angels, and saints. Genuine sacred art draws man to adoration, to prayer, and to the love of God, Creator and Savior, the Holy One and Sanctifier" (2502).

This is indeed a fitting conclusion to our meditation on the Commandments since it brings us right back to where we started—to the all-holy God who desires the holiness of his people: "You shall make and keep yourselves holy, because I am holy" (Lv 11:44).

DISCUSSION QUESTIONS

Section One: Man's Vocation—Life in the Spirit
1. What must we understand before undertaking the demands of a Gospel life?

2. Why is Baptism so important for leading a moral life?

3. What elements must be included in a catechesis of Christian morality?

4. Why do we need a relationship with Jesus Christ in order to lead a moral life?

5. What is the gift of free will?

6. What is the Church's position on the human experience and free will? How does this differ from Luther's position?

7. How is "beatitude" defined?

8. Explain the difference between "freedom" and "license."

9. What three elements does a morally good act require?

10. What actions produce virtues and vices?

11. What is conscience?

12. Through what phases does conscience progress?

13. What guides us in the formation of conscience?

14. What can contribute to the breakdown of a moral conscience?

15. How do we define someone who is virtuous?

16. List and define the "cardinal" virtues.

17. How do the seven gifts and the twelve fruits of the Holy Spirit affect us?

18. What is sin?

19. Distinguish between mortal and venial sin.

20. Why must we not regard venial sin as insignificant?

21. What conclusions have been drawn about society and virtue?

22. Explain the significance of "natural law."

23. What purposes do the Old and New Laws serve?

24. What is meant by "justification"? How does it occur?

25. Define four types of grace.

26. Why are we called to lead a moral life?

Section Two: The Ten Commandments
1. Observing the Ten Commandments is the first step to holi-

ness. What is necessary to achieve holiness fully?

2. What is the significance of God's addressing believers in the singular when He gives us His "ten words" (Ten Commandments)?

3. State the Ten Commandments.

4. In what ways can we sin against faith, hope and charity, thereby sinning against the first commandment?

5. List the four acts of the virtue of religion.

6. Explain what is meant by the worship of false gods.

7. What are the sins of irreligion?

8. Name four sins that are contrary to the second commandment.

9. What are we to remember when we give a name to someone at Baptism?

10. Why did the ancient Hebrews keep the sabbath holy?

11. Why is the Christian sabbath on Sunday?

12. How are we to spend the sabbath?

13. Besides our parents, whom are we obliged to honor and respect?

14. Explain what a family is.

15. Why does the family relate to society at large?

16. What are a family's rights?

17. Define a child's duties to his/her parents.

18. What are parents' obligations to their children?

19. How are Catholics to relate to civil authority?

20. Why is human life sacred?

21. Is killing in self-defense wrong? Explain.

22. Discuss the gravity of abortion and euthanasia.

23. Why is suicide forbidden by the fifth commandment?

24. Why should we not despair of the eternal salvation of someone who has committed suicide?

25. With regard to human dignity, in what areas must we personally strive toward moderation?

26. When are organ donations and autopsies permitted?

27. Explain the Church's concept of peace.

28. What must be remembered if we are involved in armed conflicts?

29. Who is called to chastity?

30. Why should an engaged couple remain chaste?

31. What are the sins against chastity?

32. Why are homosexual acts "intrinsically disordered"?

33. In what ways does sexuality within marriage enrich the couple?

34. Why is artificial contraception wrong?

35. Why is artificial insemination considered dishonest?

36. Name THE offense against the dignity of marriage.

37. How can people "battle" against carnal lust?

38. What does a plan for fostering decency include?

39. What constitutes theft?

40. Besides theft, what are the other sins against justice?

41. Although man was given dominion over creation, his dominion is not absolute. Explain.

42. What is the proper relationship of man to animals?

43. How are we to view work?

44. In what ways can we fulfill our responsibilities toward the poor?

45. What does the tenth commandment forbid?

46. Why is envy considered a capital sin?

47. Regarding the tenth commandment, what prevents man from entering heaven? What is necessary to reach God's kingdom?

48. Must we strive always to tell the truth? Why or why not?

49. How are martyrs and the truth related?

50. What are offenses against the truth?

51. Define lying.

52. What should be the goal of journalism?

53. What is the function of sacred art?

part four:
CHRISTIAN PRAYER

And Mary said, "My soul magnifies the Lord,
and my spirit rejoices in God my savior."
Luke 1:46, 47

part four:
CHRISTIAN PRAYER

Many people have observed that one of the principal problems with the contemporary Church is not our ecclesiology, not our morality, not our liturgy; it is the fact that most Catholics (yes, even practicing Catholics) have forgotten how to pray, many of the younger generation never even learned in the first place, and all too many across the board confuse "praying" with "saying prayers." This last section of the catechism attempts to correct that difficulty.

SECTION ONE: PRAYER IN THE CHRISTIAN LIFE

So, what is prayer? "Prayer is the raising of one's mind and heart to God or the requesting of good things from God" (2590). Those raised on the Baltimore Catechism will think they are reading a re-cycled response from that venerable text, but it's actually much older than that, coming as it does from the pen of the great Eastern Father, St. John Damascene.

Prayer in the Scriptures

That definition is all-encompassing and serves as a wonderful backdrop for a review of prayer as taught and practiced in the Hebrew Scriptures. Special attention is paid to the Psalter, summarized thus: "The Psalms constitute the masterwork of prayer in the Old Testament. They present two inseparable qualities: the personal and the communal. They extend to all dimensions of history, recalling God's promises already fulfilled and looking for the coming of the Messiah" (2596). And then a particularly strong case is made for them, as we read, "Prayed and fulfilled in Christ, the Psalms are an essential and permanent element of the prayer of the Church. They are suitable for men of every condition and time" (2597), which helps explain the equally strong plea for a deeper appreciation for the Liturgy of the Hours, found in the Worship section (cf. 1174-78).

The Christological aspect of the Psalter becomes the ideal lead-in for insights into the prayer of Jesus himself. In a most tender (and logical) reflection, we are asked to consider how Jesus must have learnt to pray from his blessed Mother (2599). Of course, many will not be surprised at that thought since they heard Archbishop Fulton Sheen quote the poem of Father Faber so often: "Lovely lady, dressed in blue, teach us how to pray; when God was just your Boy, you showed Him the way." This type of *obiter dictum* is a good indicator of how Catholic theology all hangs together; in this instance, the theology of prayer is connected to a true commitment to a full-throated affirmation of the depths of the divine condescension in the Incarnation—God-in-the-flesh had to learn how to pray!

The Gospel according to St. Luke is offered as a powerful source for teachings on prayer, wherein we discover Jesus at prayer most frequently and also giving intensive instruction in methods and attitudes of prayer. By following the pattern set by the Master of prayer, we realize that Christian prayer needs to take in the following components: conversion, faith, filial boldness. Encouraging us to pray to Jesus for what we need, the catechism stresses the power and willingness of Christ— even during his earthly life and ministry—to grant what was asked of him by those in need. The New Testament data on prayer would be incomplete were the prayer of the Blessed Virgin omitted. In her *fiat* ("Let it be done to me according to thy word") and in her *Magnificat* ("My soul magnifies the Lord, and my spirit rejoices in God my Savior"), Our Lady is identi- fied "by the generous offering of her whole being in faith" (2622) and thus serves as an example most worthy of emulation.

Prayer in the Church

The text reminds us that as the Church awaited the coming of the Holy Spirit, she was first taught how to pray—the Spirit's first real gift to the Church, as it were (2633). The various forms which prayer can take are discussed. The acronym so many of us learned as children is still helpful: ACTS—Adoration; Con- trition; Thanksgiving; Supplication. In an age so given over to the "practical," a good review of the meaning and purpose of adoration is not out of place. "*Adoration* is the first attitude of man acknowledging that he is a creature before his Creator. It exalts the greatness of the Lord who made us and the almighty power of the Savior who sets us free from evil. Adoration is homage of the spirit to the 'King of Glory,' respectful silence in the presence of the 'ever greater' God. Adoration of the thrice- holy and sovereign God of love blends with humility and gives assurance to our supplications" (2628). That profound analy- sis may contain the key to unlock the mystery and joy of prayer for countless people of goodwill who just seem incapable of entering into the experience of prayer.

We are not amazed to see the Eucharist put forth as the pinnacle of all prayer, since "the Eucharist contains and expresses all forms of prayer: it is 'the pure offering' of the whole Body of Christ to the glory of God's name and, according to the traditions of East and West, it is the 'sacrifice of praise'" (2643).

Sources of Prayer

Where does prayer originate? Christians learn about prayer from the Tradition of the Church, through the Word of God in Sacred Scripture, and in the sacred liturgy. Prayer is also taught by a lively cultivation of the theological virtues of faith, hope and charity.

Christian prayer is Trinitarian, but it "is primarily addressed to the Father; it can also be directed toward Jesus, particularly by the invocation of his holy name" (2680). Once more, reference is made to the Holy Spirit as the inspirer of prayer within a believer and as worthy of prayer as a member of the Godhead. The place of Mary in Catholic prayer is also noted, namely, that we pray with her (since she is a member of the Church with us) and to her (because of her preeminence) (2682).

Guides for Prayer

A most practical section, these short paragraphs offer a primer in prayer, giving us the who, where, when and how of the process.

Who are good models of prayer? "The *Christian family,*" ordained ministers, consecrated religious, catechists, prayer groups and spiritual directors (2685-90).

Where might one pray? Anywhere, of course, but as human beings we resonate to overtures of prayer better in some places than in others. Therefore, the catechism highlights the impor-

PART FOUR: CHRISTIAN PRAYER

tance of prayer in churches, especially where the Blessed Sacrament is reserved. Also helpful for some people is a personal "prayer corner," as well as visits to monasteries or pilgrimages (2691).

When should one pray? Taking off on St. Paul's injunction to "pray always," the text wisely notes that "we cannot pray 'at all times' if we do not pray at specific times" (2697). Therefore, it is necessary to commit oneself to daily prayer, to prayer in conjunction with the rhythms of the liturgy and the liturgical cycle, taking special account of the Liturgy of the Hours and, of course, the Sunday Eucharist.

How should one pray? The catechism provides an excellent exposition of the different methods of prayer—vocal, meditative, contemplative—making clear that the last two are not reserved for cloistered nuns but should be seen as feasible and desirable for all Christians.

In a most realistic and pastoral contribution, the text deals with "the battle of prayer" (2753), offering practical suggestions for overcoming such obstacles. In this context, one is reminded of the sage observation of Blaise Pascal that "the desire to pray is prayer."

This marvelous introduction to prayer concludes with a fine treatment on the need for filial trust that "is put to the test when we feel that our prayer is not always heard" (2756). This is the perfect preface to a meditation on the Lord's Prayer.

SECTION TWO: THE LORD'S PRAYER: "OUR FATHER!"

Following the pattern of the Roman catechism from the Council of Trent, the present work likewise ends up with a meditation on the Lord's Prayer, what Tertullian, an Early Church theologian, termed "the summary of the entire Gospel." First, we are presented with a rationale for considering this prayer central to Christian spirituality, and it is nothing less than this: "The prayer that comes to us from Jesus is truly unique . . . the only Son gives us the words the Father gave him" (2765). This is obviously in response to those who would argue either that this prayer is a construct of the Early Church or that its contemporary usefulness can be questioned. At the same time, we are warned about its proper use: "Jesus does not give us a formula to repeat mechanically" (2766). The devout recitation of this prayer inserts us into the entire Tradition of the Church as we learn from the *Didache* that from her earliest days the Church prayed this composition of Our Lord three times a day, just as the Jews prayed the venerable "Eighteen Benedictions." The Lord's Prayer has also always formed part of the Divine Office, the Sacraments of Baptism and Confirmation and, of course, the Eucharistic Sacrifice (2767-70). A last preliminary remark notes the "eschatological" nature of this prayer, that is, that it is eminently suited for the "end-time" or "the time of salvation that began with the outpouring of the Holy Spirit and will be fulfilled with the Lord's return" (2771).

Pondering the words themselves begins with a comment on the liturgical text used to introduce the Lord's Prayer. In Latin, the assembly is urged to remember that what they are about to say is incredibly bold, and so, "we *dare* to say . . . Our Father . . ." The English text obliterates that notion by suggesting that all we really need is "confidence." The only way we can utter these words, however, is through the grace of Christ; in other words, we do not speak to God in this manner by natural right but only by virtue of our supernatural adoption in Christ and the Holy Spirit (2782). This stirs up within us what the catechism identifies as "filial trust, joyous assurance, humble boldness, the certainty of being loved" (2778)—all gifts of God to his dear children redeemed by his divine Son.

Our Father

"The first phrase of the Our Father is a blessing of adoration before it is a supplication" (2781). In this word, "we give him thanks for having revealed his name to us, for the gift of believing in it, and for the indwelling of his Presence in us" (2781). The catechism teaches that our ability to relate to God as our Father is rooted in our having been reborn and adopted; thus, this is not a natural right or capacity but one conferred by grace. Hence, "the free gift of adoption requires on our part continual conversion and *new life*," with the development of two basic dispositions: "*the desire to become like him* [Christ]" and "*a humble and trusting heart* that enables us 'to turn and become like children'" (Mt 18:3) (2784-85).

It is significant that the text does not engage in the least those who argue that there are problems for some in addressing God as "Father." The implicit answer is that this mode of address is divinely revealed and those who have such difficulties need to reflect on what their problems are with the very fundamental notions of Christian revelation, Tradition and the deposit of faith.

In appending the adjective "our" to "Father," it is not a question of "express[ing] a possession, but an entirely new relationship with God" (2786). More to the point, in this manner "we are invoking the new covenant in Jesus Christ, communion with the Holy Trinity, and the divine love which spreads through the Church to encompass the world" (2801). In an ecumenical key, the text observes that "in spite of the divisions among Christians," this prayer to "'our' Father" presents "an urgent summons for all the baptized" to work for the unity of all believers (2791). We are also reminded that the use of "our" is an invitation for us to "leave individualism behind" since "if we are to it say truthfully, our divisions and oppositions have to be overcome" (2792). This Father whom we invoke is "'in heaven,'" which—more than a place—is "a way of being" (2794) or, better yet, "God's majesty and his presence in the hearts of the just. Heaven, the Father's house, is the true homeland toward which we are heading and to which, already, we belong" (2802).

This prayer continues with seven petitions (remember, St. Matthew as a Jew writing for Jews would have considered seven to be the symbol of perfection; therefore, we have in reality the perfect prayer). With great insight, the catechism says that "the first series of petitions carries us toward him [God], for his own sake: *thy* name, *thy* kingdom, *thy* will! It is characteristic of love to think first of the one whom we love" (2804). Similarly, we do not directly impose ourselves into these; we simply ask that these be done. The "second series" concerns us and our welfare, and so we find the pronoun "us" in evidence throughout.

God's Name, Kingdom and Will

When we pray, "hallowed be thy name," we are not asking that this be accomplished, for it already is. Rather, we are seeking the recognition of that holiness "by us and in us, in every nation and in each man" (2858). The "Kingdom" spoken of in the next petition, again, is not concerned with a geographical location but with the rule or dominion of God over men's minds and hearts. Therefore, "[this] refers primarily to the final coming of the reign of God through Christ's return." Very quickly, the text adds, however, that this desire (for the final consummation) does not distract the Church from her mission in this world, but engages her more fully in it (2818). To bring about God's Kingdom here on earth and to look forward to its final fulfillment suggests "a decisive battle has been joined between 'the flesh' and the Spirit" (2819). And then directing advice toward those who have a predominantly or even completely *this-worldly* approach to questions of justice and peace, the catechism says: "By a discernment according to the Spirit, Christians have to distinguish between the growth of the Reign of God and the progress of the culture and society in which they are involved. This distinction is not a separation. Man's vocation to eternal life does not suppress, but actually reinforces, his duty to put into action in this world the energies and means received from the Creator to serve justice and peace" (2820).

As we ask for God's will to be done "on earth as it is in heaven" (2822), we must really unite our voices to that of Jesus, "[for it is] in Christ, and through his human will, the will of the Father has been perfectly fulfilled once for all" (2824). And just what is his Will? The accomplishment of "his plan of salvation in the life of the world" (2860).

Bread, Forgiveness, Deliverance from Temptation and Evil

With the fourth petition, we move into concerns specifically related to human affairs. The "give us" has the ring of "filial trust" to it. "'Our daily bread' refers to the earthly nourishment necessary to everyone for subsistence, and also to the Bread of Life: the Word of God and the Body of Christ. It is received in God's 'today,' as the indispensable, (super-)essential nourishment of the feast of the coming Kingdom anticipated in the Eucharist" (2861). This desire for bread also has a necessary social dimension, demanding an effective "responsibility toward their brethren, both in their personal behavior and in their solidarity with the human family" (2831). The fact that the bread we seek is "our" bread is likewise a reminder that this loaf is "'one' loaf for the 'many,'" which expects that we "share both material and spiritual goods, not by coercion but out of love" (2833). As important as attending to the famines of the world is, the catechism does not hesitate to call our attention to an even greater and more pressing hunger in the world for the Word of God, that Word which is Jesus Christ in the Eucharist (2835).

Next we pray for forgiveness with the understanding that our willingness to be forgiving toward others is the pre-condition for our reception of mercy, so that this prayer can "[transform] the disciple by configuring him to his Master" (2844). We are warned that the mercy we desire "can penetrate our hearts only if we have learned to forgive our enemies, with the example and help of Christ" (2862).

The traditional English translation of the Lord's Prayer offers a special problem with the sixth petition, "Lead us not into temptation." The catechism even acknowledges the difficulty of properly translating the Greek original here and holds that a correct understanding involves ideas like "do not allow us to enter into temptation" or "do not let us yield to temptation" (2846). It goes on to explain that we need the Holy Spirit to enable us "[to] *discern* between trials, which are necessary for the growth of the inner man, and temptation" (2847). Furthermore, in this line we are asking the Holy Spirit to give us "the grace of vigilance and final perseverance" (2863).

"Deliver us from evil" is also critical to understand in a theologically precise manner. Our prayer is not merely for release from some abstract evil force or power abroad in the world. It concerns "a person, Satan, the Evil One, the angel who opposes God. The devil (*dia-bolos*) is the one who 'throws himself across' God's plan and his work of salvation accomplished in Christ" (2851). This is a very clear teaching aimed at some theologians who have argued against the existence of a true, personal spirit of evil, rather than a vague malevolent force. In even sharper relief, we read that this petition seeks release "from all evils, present, past, and future, of which he is the author or instigator" (2854).

The Concluding Doxology

The meditation on the Lord's Prayer concludes with a passage on the doxology attached to it in the Byzantine tradition: "'For the kingdom, the power and the glory are yours, now and forever." The three realities thus attributed to God are exactly what the Devil had promised to Christ (cf. Lk 4:5-6). Christ, on the other hand, "restores them to his Father and our Father, until he hands over the kingdom to him when the mystery of salvation will be brought to its completion and God will be all in all" (2855). The catechism ends with the words of St. Cyril of Jerusalem on the Lord's Prayer: "Then, after the prayer is over you say 'Amen,' which means 'So be it,' thus ratifying with our 'Amen' what is contained in the prayer that God has taught us" (2856).

A TOUR OF THE CATHOLIC CATECHISM

DISCUSSION QUESTIONS

Section One: Prayer in the Christian Life

1. How does praying involve more than just "saying prayers"?

2. Who first described prayer as "the raising of one's mind and heart to God or the requesting of good things from God"?

3. Why do the Psalms of the Hebrew Scriptures occupy such a central place in the Church's liturgy?

4. What do the Gospels—in particular, St. Luke's—teach us about the ingredients of authentic prayer?

5. What are the four *kinds* (not methods) of prayer traditionally presented in catechesis?

6. Explain how Holy Mass is *the* consummate prayer.

7. Explain the place of the Saints, especially the Blessed Virgin Mary, in Christian prayer.

8. Identify some of the different *methods* of prayer.

9. A lax Catholic justifies his absence from Mass with the claim, "I can pray better at home, or while taking a walk in the woods." Respond to this excuse.

10. People nowadays are pulled in so many directions by the demands of family, work, etc. How can busy Christians take seriously St. Paul's injunction to "pray always"?

Section Two: The Lord's Prayer

1. Why is the Lord's Prayer central to our faith?

2. In what liturgies does the Lord's Prayer have an integral part?

3. How can we dare address God as our "Father"?

4. What is the significance of the word "Our"?

5. Why might the Lord's Prayer be considered a "perfect prayer"?

6. Explain how the first three petitions in the Lord's Prayer are directed toward God's glory.

7. What do we mean when we refer to "our daily bread"?

8. What must we do to receive God's forgiveness?

9. When we petition God not to lead us into temptation, what are we really asking?

10. What is "evil"?

11. Explain the significance of our "Amen."

conclusion:
THE SENSE OF THE SACRED

Permit me to offer some summarizing remarks we can make about this pillar of the Catholic Faith. Certain themes recur throughout the discussion on the Church's sacramental life.

1. Again and again, we discover an effort to restore a sense of the sacred by emphasizing the primacy of the spiritual and the supernatural. Don't miss, for example, the regular use of words like "holy" and "saint."

2. In response to a resurgence of a virulent strain of neo-Pelagianism in contemporary catechetics, moral theology and liturgy, the catechism stresses the absolute and indispensable necessity for divine grace. In other words, we cannot work out our salvation on our own; it is God and God alone who accomplishes the task of salvation.

3. In an era which has witnessed what the present Holy Father has characterized as the "clericalization of the laity and the laicization of the clergy," repeatedly we come across passages that highlight the intimate connection between the min-

isterial priesthood and the sacraments.

4. So many of the post-conciliar abuses in all areas of ecclesial life have developed because of the tendency to put flesh on what Voltaire once pilloried when he quipped, "God made man in His own image and likeness, and man has never ceased to return the compliment." This catechism is unmistakably Christo-centric, rather than anthropocentric.

5. The text is as comfortable in quoting St. John Chrysostom as it is the documents of Vatican II, thereby demonstrating the continuity of Catholic theology down the ages, that Faith which St. Augustine lovingly spoke of as a beauty "so ancient and yet so new."

6. Notice the very common use of the present tense, as we read that "Christ says" or "the apostles do," thus serving as constant reminders of the on-going presence of Christ and the apostles in the Church today, so that we are not dealing with events from a distant past but very much from contemporary— indeed, eternal—realities.

In short, I believe we have been given a document that historians will cite as beginning in a serious manner the renewal envisioned and mandated by the Second Vatican Council. It reclaims the Council for the whole Church—the Church of Tradition—thus putting the lie to assertions that Vatican II sought to create a new Faith and a new Church.

Perhaps a generation raised on the truths so clearly enunciated here will be able to read better and more effectively "the signs of the times." And so, such young people will be able to lead modern man to the God who "became man that men might become gods," having recourse to the sacraments as the God-given means to bring about that noble and lofty goal of divinizing the human race—but doing it God's way, instead of our own.

appendix
HELPS FOR PRAYER AND STUDY

PRAYERS FOR ENLIGHTENMENT AND AID

Two Prayers to the Holy Spirit

Come Holy Spirit, come by means of the powerful intercession of the Immaculate Heart of Mary, your well-beloved
spouse.

———

Come Holy Spirit, fill the hearts of your faithful, and en-
kindle in us the fire of your divine love. Send forth your
spirit and we will be recreated, and you will renew the face of
the earth.

O God, who instructed the hearts of the faithful by the light
of your divine Spirit, grant us by that same spirit to be truly
wise and to rejoice in your holy consolation through the same
Christ, our Lord. Amen

St. Ignatius' Prayer of Abandonment

Take, O Lord, my liberty. Receive my memory, my understanding, my imagination, my entire will. All that I am
and possess, you have bestowed on me. I want to give it back
to you and be entirely subject to your divine will. Only grant

me your love and grace. With these I am rich enough and I desire nothing more. Amen.

Memorare

R emember, O most gracious Virgin Mary, that never was it known that anyone who fled to your protection, implored your help or sought your intercession was left unaided.

Inspired by this confidence, I fly to you, O Virgin of virgins, my mother. To you I come, before you I stand sinful and sorrowful.

O Mother of the Word Incarnate, despise not my petitions but in your mercy hear and anwer me. Amen.

Miraculous Medal Prayer of St. Maximilian Kolbe

O Mary, conceived without sin, pray for us who have recourse to you, and for all those who do not have recourse to you, especially the enemies of the Holy Church and those most in need of your mercy. Amen.

Oldest Prayer to St. Joseph

S t. Joseph, whose protection is so great, so strong, so prompt before the throne of God, I place in you all my interests and desires. Do assist me by your powerful intercession and obtain for me, from your divine Son, all spiritual blessings, through Christ, our Lord. Amen.

St. Michael Prayer of Pope Leo XIII

S t. Michael the Archangel, defend us in battle, be our protection against the wickedness and snares of the devil. May God rebuke him, we humbly pray. And do thou, O prince of the heavenly host, by the power of God, cast into hell Satan, and all the evil spirits, who prowl through the world seeking the ruin of souls. Amen.

Fatima Daily Offering
O my Jesus, I offer this for love of you, for the conversion of poor sinners, and in reparation for sins committed against the Immaculate Heart of Mary. Amen.

Prayer for the Pope
Holy Spirit, source of all gifts, give to your shepherd, the Pope, a spirit of courage and right judgement, a spirit of knowledge and love.

Holy Spirit, help your Pope to govern with fidelity those entrusted to his care. May he, as successor to the apostle Peter, and Vicar of Christ, build your Church into a sacrament of unity, love and peace for all the world. We ask this through the hearts of Jesus and Mary. Amen.

The Ten Commandments
1. I am the Lord your God. You shall honor no other god but me.
2. You shall not misuse the name of the Lord, your God.
3. You shall keep holy the Sabbath.
4. You shall honor your father and mother.
5. You shall not kill.
6. You shall not commit adultery.
7. You shall not steal.
8. You shall not bear false witness against your neighbor.
9. You shall not covet your neighbor's wife.
10. You shall not covet your neighbor's goods.

The Seven Sacraments
Baptism
Reconciliation
Eucharist

Confirmation
Marriage
Holy Orders
Anointing of the Sick

Six Laws of the Church
Attend Mass on Sundays and holy days of obligation.
Confess your sins at least once a year.
Receive the Eucharist at least during the Easter season.
Keep holy the holy days of obligation.
Observe the prescribed days of fasting and abstinence.
Contribute to the material needs of the Church.

Theological Virtues
Faith
Hope
Love

Cardinal Virtues
Prudence
Justice
Fortitude
Temperance

Seven Capital Sins
Pride
Covetousness
Lust
Anger
Gluttony
Envy
Sloth

Gifts of the Holy Spirit (Isaiah 11:2, 3)
Wisdom
Understanding
Counsel
Knowledge
Fortitude
Piety
Fear of the Lord

Fruits of the Holy Spirit (Galatians 5:22, 23)
Charity
Joy
Peace
Patience
Kindness
Goodness
Faithfulness
Humility
Self-control

Spiritual Works of Mercy
To admonish the sinner
To instruct the ignorant
To counsel the doubtful
To comfort the sorrowful
To bear wrongs patiently
To forgive all injuries
To pray for the living and the dead

Corporal Works of Mercy
To feed the hungry
To give drink to the thirsty

To clothe the naked
To visit the imprisoned
To shelter the homeless
To visit the sick
To bury the dead

Holy Days of Obligation
January 1—Solemnity of Mary, Mother of God
Forty days after Easter—Ascension Thursday
August 15—Feast of Mary's Assumption
November 1—All Saints' Day
December 8—Solemnity of the Immaculate Conception
December 25—Christmas Day

ARE YOU "UNDER THE MANTLE" OF MARY?

The purpose of the Militia Immaculata of St. Maximilian Kolbe is to encourage you to give yourself entirely to Mary Immaculate through total consecration—to get "under the mantle" of her protective care. She will then be free to use you as an extraordinary instrument to bring about the spiritual conversion of others, and to bring about the reign of the Sacred Heart of Jesus.

Are you ready to get under Mary's mantle through total consecration according to St. Maximilian? Pray about it first. If the answer is yes, then do this:

1. Pick a Marian feast day to make your consecration.

2. Prepare spiritually: daily Mass if possible, pray the Rosary, spiritual reading. Go to confession within the week. Attend Mass on your consecration day and receive the Eucharist.

3. On the consecration day, before an image of Mary, make a decision to renounce all attachment to sin. You will thus be removing interior obstacles so Our Lady can make you her own in the Holy Spirit most completely.

4. Say the MI consecration prayer (next page). Pray for the Holy Father's intentions.

5. Wear the Miraculous Medal.

6. Ask Our Lady and St. Maximilian how you can best serve the Lord.

7. We also encourage you to officially enroll in the Militia Immaculata. Do this by filling out a registration form and sending it to the MI National Center, 1600 W. Park Avenue, Libertyville, IL 60048-2593. You will receive a membership certificate and a free Miraculous Medal. (Call **847-367-7800** to receive an informative MI brochure containing the registration form and consecration prayer.)

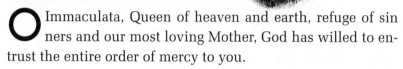

St. Maximilian's

PRAYER OF TOTAL CONSECRATION

O Immaculata, Queen of heaven and earth, refuge of sinners and our most loving Mother, God has willed to entrust the entire order of mercy to you.

I, (name), a repentant sinner, cast myself at your feet, humbly imploring you to take me with all that I am and have, wholly to yourself as your possession and property. Please make of me, of all my powers of soul and body, of my whole life, death and eternity, whatever most pleases you.

I f it pleases you, use all that I am and have without reserve, wholly to accomplish what was said of you: "She will crush your head," and "You alone have destroyed all heresies in the whole world."

L et me be a fit instrument in your immaculate and merciful hands for introducing and increasing your glory to the maximum in all the many strayed and indifferent souls, and thus help extend as far as possible the blessed kingdom of the most Sacred Heart of Jesus. For wherever you enter, you obtain the grace of conversion and growth in holiness, since it is through your hands that all graces come to us from the most Sacred Heart of Jesus.

V. Allow me to praise you, O Holy Virgin.
R. Give me strength against your enemies.

MAJOR WRITINGS OF THE MODERN POPES
PRESENT-1846

Pope John Paul II (1978-)
Encyclical letters

1979 *Redemptor Hominis* (On the redemption and dignity of the human race)

1980 *Dives in Misericordia* (On the rich mercy of God)

1981 *Laborem Exercens* (On the value and dignity of human work)

1985 *Slavorum Apostoli* (Commemorating the life and work of Sts. Cyril and Methodius, evangelists of the Slavs)

1986 *Dominum et Vivificantem* (On the Holy Spirit in the life of the Church and the world)

1987 *Redemptoris Mater* (On the role of Mary in the mystery of Christ and the life of the Church and the world)
Sollicitudo Rei Socialis (On social concerns on the twentieth anniversary of Pope Paul VI's *Populorum Progressio*)

1991 *Redemptoris Missio* (On the permanent validity of the Church's missionary mandate)
Centesimus Annus (Commemorating the one hundredth anniversary of Pope Leo XIII's *Rerum Novarum* and addressing contemporary social questions)

1993 *Veritatis Splendor* (Exposition of the Church's moral teaching)

1995 *Evangelium Vitae* (Church's teaching on life issues)

1995 *Ut Unum Sint* (On the need for ecumenical commitment and Christian unity)

Apostolic constitutions, letters and exhortations

1979 *Catechesi Tradendae* (Exhortation on Catholic catechesis)

1980 *Dominicae Cenae* (Letter on Eucharistic worship)

1981 *Familiaris Consortio* (Exhortation on the family)

1981 *Sacrae Disciplinae Leges* (Apostolic constitution—preamble to the Code of Canon Law)

1984 *Salvifici Doloris* (Letter on the value of human suffering)
Redemptionis Donum (Exhortation on religious life)
Reconciliatio et Paenitentia (Exhortation on personal and social sin)

1988 *Mulieris Dignitatem* (Letter on the dignity and vocation of women)
Vicesimus Quintus Annus (Letter on liturgy and culture)

1989 *Christifideles Laici* (Exhortation on the Catholic laity)

1992 *Pastores Dabo Vobis* (Exhortation on the formation of priests)

1994 *Tertio Millennio Adveniente* (Letter preparing for the jubilee year 2000 and the third millennium)
Fidei Depositum (Apostolic constitution—preamble to the *Catechism of the Catholic Church*)
Ordinatio Sacerdotalis (Letter on the ordination of women)
Letter to Families (Commemorating Year of the Family)

1995 *Orientale Lumen* (Letter on the Eastern Orthodox Churches)
To the World's Women (Letter anticipating the UN World Conference on Women in Bejing, China)

To obtain the documents of John Paul II, and selected ones by other popes, contact:
Pauline Books and Media
50 St. Paul's Ave.
Boston, MA 02130
800-876-4463

A TOUR OF THE CATHOLIC CATECHISM

CNS Documentary Service
3211 Fourth St. N.E.,Washington, D.C. 20017-1100
202-541-3290

Selected Books
1981 *Original Unity of Man and Woman* (Catechesis on the Book of Genesis)
1983 *Blessed Are the Pure of Heart* (Catechesis on the Sermon on the Mount and the writings of St. Paul)
1984 *Reflections on Humanae Vitae* (Catechesis on the morality and spirituality of marriage)
1994 *Crossing the Threshold of Hope* (Presents Holy Father's beliefs on faith, human dignity, hope and eternal life)
Prayers and Devotions (Daily meditation manual excerpted from Holy Father's writings)
The Jeweler's Shop (Early play on marriage)
1995 *Breakfast with the Pope* (120 daily meditations)

Pope Paul VI (1963-1978)
1964 *Ecclesiam Suam* (On the Church)
1965 *Mysterium Fidei* (On the Holy Eucharist)
1967 *Populorum Progressio* (On the development of peoples)
1968 *Humanae Vitae* (On human life issues and regulation of birth)
1975 *Evangelii Nuntiandi* (On evangelization of the nations)

Pope John XXIII (1958-1963)
1959 *Ad Petri Cathedram* (On truth, unity and peace in the spirit of charity)
1961 *Mater et Magistra* (On Christianity and social progress)
1963 *Pacem in Terris* (On establishing universal peace and liberty)

Pope Pius XII (1939-1958)

1943 *Mystici Corporis Christi* (On the mystical body of Christ)
Divino Afflante Spiritu (On promoting biblical studies)
1947 *Mediator Dei* (On reforming the liturgy)
1950 *Munificentissimus Deus* (Dogmatic definition of Mary's Assumption)
1950 *Humani Generis* (On attempts to distort Catholic truths)
1954 *Ad Caeli Reginam* (On the queenship of Mary)

Pope Pius XI (1922-1939)

1925 *Quas Primas* (Instituting Feast of Christ the King)
1930 *Casti Connubii* (On Christian marriage)
1931 *Quadragesimo Anno* (Commemorating fortieth anniversary of Leo XII's *Rerum Novarum*; on reconstructing the social order)
1937 *Divini Redemptoris* (On atheistic communism)
1937 *Mit Brennender Sorge* (Denouncing Nazism and anti-Christian ideologies)

Pope Benedict XV (1914-1922)

1914 *Ad Beatissimi Apostolorum* (Appeal for peace [on advent of WWI])
1917 *Humani Generis Redemptionem* (On preaching the word of God)
Published revised Code of Canon Law
1920 *Pacem, Dei Munus Pulcherrimum* (On peace and Christian reconciliation [on conclusion of WWI])

Pope St. Pius X (1903-1914)

1904 *Ad Diem Illum Laetissimum* (On the Immaculate Conception)
1907 *Lamentabili* (Condemnation of Modernism)

Pascendi Dominici Gregis (On the doctrines of Modernism)

Pope Leo XIII (1878-1903)

1879 *Aeterni Patris* (On the philosophy of St. Thomas Aquinas)
1880 *Arcanum* (On Christian Marriage)
1884 *Humanum Genus* (On Freemasonry)
1891 *Rerum Novarum* (On capitol, labor and social issues)
1892 *Inimica Vis* (On Freemasonry)
1893 *Providentissimus Deus* (On the study of Holy Scripture)
1896 *Apostolicae Curae* (On the validity of Anglican orders)
1899 *Annum Sacrum* (On consecration to the Sacred Heart)
1902 *Mira Caritatis* (On the Holy Eucharist)

Pope Pius IX (1846-1878)

1846 *Qui Pluribus* (On faith and religion)
1854 *Ineffabilis Deus* (Dogmatic definition of Mary's Immaculate Conception)
1864 *Quanta Cura* (Condemnation of harmful liberal ideas)
1870 *Pastor Aeternus* (Vatican I document defining papal infallibility)

THE TWENTY-ONE ECUMENICAL COUNCILS
OF THE CATHOLIC CHURCH

325 **Nicaea I** (Convened to resolve Arian crisis. *Homoousios* inserted into what became "Nicene" Creed. Fixed date of Easter.)
381 **Constantinople I** (Sought to heal divisiveness of Arianism. Expanded and ratified Nicene Creed.)
431 **Ephesus** (Sought to end Nestorian controversy. De-

clared Mary "Mother of God.")

451 **Chalcedon** (Affirmed orthodox doctrine of Christ's divine and human natures.)

553 **Constantinople II** (Condemned Nestorianism and Three Chapters.)

680 **Constantinople III** (Condemned Monothelitism and reaffirmed Chalcedon on two natures of Christ.)

787 **Nicaea II** (Sought to resolve Iconoclastic controversy.)

869-70 **Constantinople IV** (Excommunicated Eastern patriarch Photius. Widened gulf between Eastern and Western Churches.)

1123 **Lateran I** (Ended Investiture conflicts by confirming Condordat of Worms.)

1139 **Lateran II** (Condemned antipope Anacletus II and schismatic followers.)

1179 **Lateran III** (Healed damage of schismatic antipope Callistus III. Provided for election of pope by College of Cardinals.)

1215 **Lateran IV** (Promulgated annual confession, Easter communion, doctrine of transubstantiation. Condemned Waldenses and Cathars.)

1245 **Lyons I** (Addressed problems of Eastern schism. Deposed Emperor Frederick II.)

1274 **Lyons II** (Addressed problems of Eastern schism and moral decline of clergy.)

1311-12 **Vienne** (Dealt with problems with Order of Knights Templar.)

1414-18 **Constance** (Ended Great Schism of 1378. High point of conciliarism with issuing of *Sacrosancta*. Condemned Hus and Wycliffe.)

1431-45 **Ferrara-Florence** (Tried to reunite Eastern and Western Churches.)

1512-17 **Lateran V** (Invalidated decrees of false Council of Pisa and launched some reforms.)

1545-63 **Trent** (Refuted errors of Protestantism and clarified Catholic teaching. Reformed clerical and religious morals and disciplines. Produced new catechism, reformed missal, updated liturgy.)

1869-70 **Vatican I** (Confirmed compatibility of faith and reason; defined doctrine of papal infallibility.)

1962-65 **Vatican II** (Convened to better prepare the Church to communicate with, and to evangelize, the modern world. Updated liturgy, Church disciplines, evangelical methods, while staying faithful to her Sacred Tradition.)

THE SIXTEEN DOCUMENTS
OF THE SECOND VATICAN COUNCIL

Lumen Gentium (Dogmatic Constitution on the Church), November 21, 1964

Dei Verbum (Dogmatic Constitution on Divine Revelation), November 18, 1964

Sacrosanctum Concilium (Constitution on the Sacred Liturgy), December 4, 1963

Gaudium et Spes (Pastoral Constitution on the Church in the Modern World), December 7, 1965

Inter Mirifica (Decree on the Instruments of Social Communication), December 4, 1963

Unitatis Redintegratio (Decree on Ecumenism), November 21, 1964

Orientalium Ecclesiarum (Decree on Eastern Catholic Churches), November 21, 1964

Christus Dominus (Decree on the Bishops' Pastoral Office in the Church), October 28, 1965

Optatam Totius (Decree on Priestly Formation), October 28, 1965

Perfectae Caritatis (Decree on the Appropriate Renewal of Religious Life), October 28, 1965

Apostolicam Actuositatem (Decree on the Apostolate of the Laity), November 18, 1965

Presbyterorum Ordinis (Decree on the Ministry and Life of Priests), December 7, 1965

Ad Gentes (Decree on the Church's Missionary Activity), December 7, 1965

Gravissimum Educationis (Declaration on Christian Education), October 28, 1965

Nostra Aetate (Declaration on the Relationship of the Church to Non-Christian Religions), October 28, 1965

Dignitatis Humanae (Declaration on Religious Freedom), December 7, 1965

Vatican Council II: The Conciliar and Post Conciliar Documents, editor Austin Flannery, OP, available from Pauline Books and Media, 800-876-4463.

A TOUR OF THE CATHOLIC CATECHISM

INDEX

A

Abortion, 8, 21, 144
Abraham, 19
Ad Gentes, 49
Adam, 53, 122
Adoration of Eucharist, 173
Adultery, 147
Agnosticism, 136
AIDS, 104
Alcohol use, 145
Almsgiving, 88
Ambrose, St., 5, 87, 88, 198
Anawim, 44, 45
Angels, 28, 29, 54, 68, 159
Apostasy, 135
Apostle's Creed, 23, 24, 53
Apostolic succession, 51, 65
Aquinas, St. Thomas, 7, 24, 92, 124, 136, 143, 157
Ark of the Covenant, 136
Art, 159
Ascension, 38-40
Astrology, 136
Athanasian Creed, 26
Atheism, 136
Augustine, St., 5, 7, 18, 24, 45, 124, 132, 146, 158, 184
Avarice, 155, 156

B

Baltimore Catechism, 159
Baptism, *71-76;* and Trinity, 25, 42, 43, 50; effects, 31, 37, 38, 49, 53, 54, 75; infant, 73; and penance, 87; and priesthood, 92; and sacramentals, 107; and morality, 117; Christian name, 136, 137
Basil, St., 29
Beatitudes, 121
Beauty, 159
Bellarmine, Robert, 5
Blasphemy, 136
Blessings, 107
Boasting, 157

Borromeo, St. Charles, 5

C

Calumny, 157
Canisius, St. Peter, 5
Capital punishment, 143
Capitalism, 154
Catechesi Tradendae, 4, 6, 32, 35
Catechesis, 4, 5, 7-10, 12; experiential, 4, 8; and sacramentals, 79
Catechism of Catholic Church; purpose, 3-12; structure, 8-10; proper use, 11, 12
Catechumenate, 72
Catholic Church, *47-58;* renewal, 3, 5, 184; source of truth, 4, 9, 12; conservative and liberal, 12, 48; "cafeteria" Catholicism, 22; mother, 133
Celibacy, 96, 98
Chastity, 148-152
Chrysostom, St. John, 5, 54, 98, 137, 155, 184
Cicero, 130
Code of Canon Law, 136
Commandments, Ten, 4, *134-159;* and love, 134; First, 135, 136; Second, 136, 137; Third, 137, 138; Fourth, 138-143; Fifth, 143-147; Sixth and Ninth, 147-152; Seventh and Tenth, 152-156; Eighth, 156-159
Communion of Saints, 52
Communism, 19, 154
Concupiscence, 87, 151, 152
Confessions of St. Augustine, 7
Confirmation, 43, *76-81*
Congregation for the Doctrine of the Faith, 143
Conscience, 125, 126
Constitution on the Sacred Liturgy, 63
Contraception, 5, 8, 21, 101, 150, 151
Conversion, 87, 88, 126, 128, 131, 171

202

This Is Marytown

Marytown, with its shrine to St. Maximilian Kolbe and historic Eucharistic adoration chapel, is operated by the Conventual Franciscan Friars of Marytown, St. Bonaventure Province.

An important ministry of the friars is promoting the principles and programs of the Militia Immaculata (MI or Knights of the Immaculata). The MI is a worldwide evangelization movement founded by St. Maximilian Kolbe in 1917 that encourages a total consecration to the Blessed Virgin Mary as a means of spiritual renewal for individuals and society.

To do this work, the friars have their own *Immaculata* magazine, Marytown Press, a religious gift store and a print shop. They hold regular educational programs and liturgical services, and welcome prayer groups and organizations to meet on the premises. A twenty-four room retreat wing will house overnight guests and be available for private and directed retreats in 1997.

Directed tours of the adoration chapel and Kolbe shrine are gladly arranged. Call **847-367-7800** for more information about Marytown's many ministries, or send in the form below.

- -

Please send me information about St. Maximilian Kolbe and Marytown's many ministries.

Name _____

Address _____

City/State/Zip _____

Phone _____

(Mail to Marytown, 1600 W. Park Ave., Libertyville, IL 60048-2593)